33 Ways to Improve in Business and Life

Ronald Myer

Peak Capital Inc

ISBN: 979-8-9874060-2-1 (hardcover)
ISBN: 979-8-9874060-0-7 (paperback)
ISBN: 979-8-9874060-9-0 (ebook)

DEDICATION

I was privileged by having a coach in my house every day growing up. My mom, Dr. Darlis Myer, was a coach for corporations as well as a marriage and individual counselor. I received the same advice and lessons those corporations and individuals received. From a very young age I was taught many virtues by her:

- How to recognize and respect different types of personalities
- The importance of integrity and always maintaining your values
- To appreciate different perspectives
- How to make others more successful
- To set dreams and goals and go after them

I was instilled with self-confidence at a young age when most kids are trying to find their way, and at the same time the need to maintain humility. I was provided a foundation of a Christian upbringing. Mom always showed an interest in me as a person and as a businessman. We often talk about how life is going and how each of the businesses are doing. That includes our 30-year tradition of me getting a free haircut while I tell her how work is going.

Mom has been a great resource and always there for me. This book could not have been written without her, as I would not have learned and recognized the importance of many of the concepts captured here. Thank you, Mom, for all you have done to support my success.

TABLE OF CONTENTS

BEYOND THE DESK

INTRODUCTION

I started writing this book 20 years ago. As I progressed through my career, I developed concepts I believed were not talked about enough, ideas I felt other popular leadership and self-growth books were missing. After every valuable experience, thought, and conversation, I began writing coinciding chapter ideas. When it came time to flesh them out, it felt natural and fairly easy to complete because I had already been living these business principles.

What surprised me was how each idea still held value even decades later. Some of these concepts are unique though others have not yet received enough focus in the field. Because each chapter is independent in its topic and message, this book is more of a collection of articles than a traditional business book. Focusing on the ones you are drawn to and skipping over others does not take away from what the work offers. Each chapter can stand independently.

Even though some concepts are described in an office setting and others elsewhere, you will find that their application fits more than just one environment. Whether at work, at home, serving on a school committee, or involved in a volunteer organization, this book will lead to a better, more successful life if you take time to truly digest it.

The chapters are intentionally brief, without a lot of fluff. I always enjoy the CliffNotes® of a self-help book more than actually reading it cover to cover. Hence, each chapter has introductory bullet points and a challenge question at the end.

This book is not meant to promote general ideas but instead, provide steps you can implement today to change your attitude and actions positively. Some ideas may not yet apply at this stage of your life, but will become critical at another. If you want to rate yourself, year after year, on how well you have implemented certain concepts, you can easily re-read those chapters.

I find it easy to read a book or attend a seminar, thinking, I really like and agree with what was said, but weeks later, still need to change any attitudes or behaviors. This is why I have created a simple checklist you can use periodically to measure how well you are utilizing the concepts in this book.

Download the checklist at:
PeakCapitalCompany.com/33WaysBook

I encourage you to set a specific month each year for its review. You can also provide the list to someone else and have them rate you on your adoption of the concepts. How you score is different from what is important though. Improvement is what matters.

The book has something for everyone, with chapters on:

- A unique time management tool (Chapter 1)

- How to make decisions quicker and better (Chapters 2 & 3)

- The benefit of quarterly focus days (Chapter 7)

- What an ideal workday could look like (Chapter 8)

- Why no one is overworked (Chapter 9)

- When your greatest strength becomes your greatest weakness (Chapter 22)

- Why you should think you are right but assume you are wrong (Chapter 23), and

- Four steps to changing a habit (Chapter 24)

With hundreds of business and self-help books out there, I hope this one becomes your favorite because it differs from the rest. It is a quick read with tools on every page to change your life positively.

If reading a chapter impacts your life, I would love to hear about it.

Go to PeakCapitalCompany.com/33WaysBook
and fill out the comments form.

Happy reading!

BUSINESS

1
Time Management
A Post-it® Note?

Learn how a Post-it® can be used to set daily priorities.

Stay focused on critical tasks.

It is your 2"x 1.5" solution to getting the most out of your day.

Priority setting is fundamental to effective time management. However, if you find yourself failing to fully execute key responsibilities on a routine basis, I want to offer you the power of a simple Post-it note.

Start your day by listing the top 1-4 things that need to be done. Write them on a Post-it and place it somewhere clearly visible to you. I carry a Post-it note of priorities in my shirt pocket so I can physically sense that I have outstanding tasks to accomplish and can easily reference my list throughout the day.

For this strategy to work, you must commit to only head home for the day once those items on your list have been completed. I have caught myself referencing my Post-it in the mid-afternoon and realizing if I did not attend to an item, it would not get done. That meant postponing replies to emails because I had established higher priorities for the day on my Post-it that outweighed new emails received. If I did not start on the task immediately, I would either have to go home later or fail to check it off my Post-it. Before you adopt this strategy, it is important to acknowledge that no one can predict precisely how a day will unfold. Distractions are inevitable. Not everything on your Post-it will always get done. And that is okay because not all distractions are meaningless. There will be unavoidable moments where your attention is needed elsewhere, and priorities must shift, but if you streamline your Post-it to include just those few tasks that absolutely have to get done, you will learn to prioritize those and in turn, cross them off.

So what happens when it is the end of the day, and you simply cannot get to everything on your list? Then you must carry that Post-it with you into the next day or the following days. Nothing is more frustrating than having to hold on to a Post-it for days. Trust me, a wrinkly, scratched-up Post-it note is not something you want to keep carrying around. But it is motivating. When this happens, you must remind yourself that what is on the list was put there because you initially felt it was a priority. If something changes and you determine the item is no longer necessary, then by all means, remove it from the list. However, this must be a rare occurrence, otherwise, the Post-it strategy will lose value to you. The most enjoyable part about utilizing the Post-it note system is when you can throw it away because you have not only prioritized the tasks you needed to get done… you have completed them. (And you get your shirt pocket back.)

WHAT YOUR POST-IT IS NOT

Your Post-it cannot be a wish list.

The tasks on it are different from what you wish or hope to accomplish. They are the one, two, three, or four things that must be done, no matter what. If the Post-it includes a lengthy list of tasks you wish to get completed, you will consistently not complete the items within one day, which will feel frustrating and unproductive. You will develop a much higher probability of success if you keep the Post-it strategy simple and initially view what is on it with high significance and urgency.

Your Post-it should not be a large strategic project.

You cannot complete a large project in one day, so your Post-it needs to be specific to tasks you can complete today. Writing down a large project provides no focus on the next steps. It needs to provide manageable tasks. Large project milestones are reached by taking the necessary steps each day to complete the tasks for a particular stage of the project, so write down the next step.

Your Post-it is not simple tasks.

It should not include a schedule of meetings, detailed appointments or mundane and generic reminders. Instead, it needs to be a list of a few tasks that take more than a few minutes but not entire days to complete.

What Your Post-it IS

Your Post-it can include steps.

Break down large projects into steps that your Post-it list can frame. These steps can then be turned into daily action items that accomplish a significant goal through smaller, specific tasks.

Your Post-it can provide the best order to complete tasks.

By having a short list of tasks that need to be done, you can set priorities on when and how they are accomplished. For example, there have been times when I saw an uncompleted item on my list that involved communicating with a coworker. I knew I had to address that task before the end of the day, but if I waited too long, that person would be gone, and I would not be able to complete my task. In situations like this, the Post-it not only prioritizes tasks, it also helps establish time sensitivity.

Your Post-it is a personality illuminator.

If you took the Myers-Briggs Personality Test and your letters ended in TJ, you may be reading this and already mentally adopting this tool by adding "Post-its." [1] On the other hand, if you do not like being constrained by a checklist and operate better with a free-flowing schedule, you might not have been as excited with this topic, and your Myers Briggs' letters probably do not end in TJ. You can still find the Post-it useful if you identify with the latter. Instead of attempting to weave the strategy into your every day, try to utilize it only on certain days throughout the week when something must be done, and on the other days, work Post-it free. This allows you to experience the benefits of prioritizing with the Post-it without fully modifying your preferences.

As you find the right Post-it strategy, you may be surprised to discover that this method is effective when you are busy, but especially when your workload is lighter than

---

1 mbtionline.com

normal. It is a human tendency to allow a task to expand to fill all the available time. However, by pre-determining a few "must do's," you will be able to stay focused on getting things done when they need to be done without unnecessarily clouding your day.

It may be challenging to pick just two or three priorities when it feels like so much more needs to be accomplished. When I am at my busiest, I motivate myself to fill the Post-it with critical tasks to still have that feeling of accomplishment at the end of the day. Otherwise, the busyness can pull your attention in multiple directions, and you will be left not fulfilling core responsibilities that, as a result, get carried over into the night or the following day.

One or two items always need to be done within a business day. Even if it is as simple as sending someone a card, list it on your Post-it, because this tool is not meant to be exclusive to just work tasks. It is meant to refocus you in all areas of your life.

Far too easily, we have the natural inclination to delay what we need to do because of whatever is directly in front of us, such as email, TV, or social media. Hence, having those few key things that we can control and that we can get done often results in a much more relaxed and focused day with a greater sense of accomplishment.

CHALLENGE

Use this methodology three days within one week. At the end of that week, compare your emotional state and your accomplishments for those three days to the two days when you did not use a Post-it to set your critical tasks. It seems too simple to be true, but the results will speak for themselves. You will be amazed at the impact that putting a few tasks on a Post-it at the beginning of the day can have on your life, the lives of those around you, and on your business success.

"Simplicity is the ultimate
sophistication."
– Clare Boothe Luce

2

TIMING OF DECISION MAKING

What is the best thought process for making a decision?

What should be considered when making a decision?

Know when to decide immediately versus waiting.

Decisions, whether personal or professional, are always there waiting to be made. Leaders must establish a process to reach conclusions thoughtfully and effectively. However, the finality of decision-making can render the process difficult. Sometimes once a decision is made, there is no going back, and the fear of possibly choosing the wrong outcome can weigh heavily. Oftentimes people in businesses and at home neglect to think through the ramifications of a decision resulting in the avoidable consequences and stress of a negative outcome.

This chapter is not about how to reach a decision quickly. It is rather about being conscious of your decision-making process. It may sound counterintuitive to Chapter 23, "Think Right, Assume Wrong," but the two concepts work well together. When making a decision, you want to be confident that your answer is correct. However, sometimes without additional information, you may be wrong. Initially acknowledging this is important to great leadership.

Several factors influence good decision making related to timing. It is essential to learn the difference between when waiting to make a decision is appropriate and when it is better to move forward immediately. Simply delaying a decision will not make you more informed on an issue, only additional input can do that. Delaying can only be helpful if it allows you to better analyze potential outcomes or gather more facts and information. Delaying is good if it generates more communication on the topic and potentially shed light on something previously unknown or not considered.

When faced with making a decision, a key question to determine if you are ready to decide is, "Could more information impact my choice?" If delaying will not reveal any new information, then you can give yourself permission to decide and move forward. It can be incredibly freeing and give you confidence in your decision-making ability.

As you evaluate decisions, determine what information may be missing and how it can be discovered. Average leaders may think of facts that are nice to know, but great leaders discern which points will be influential and which will not. Abundant information is not always more valuable.

Sometimes not making an immediate decision is better. Delaying may be helpful when you do not have all the critical information that will impact the outcome.

True liberation for leaders is when they feel a decision can be made based on what is already known. Then, they can move forward without stressing over "what-ifs." And even if one of those alternative "what-ifs" comes true and the choice was wrong, they can accept that it is always easier to be a Monday morning quarterback than game day decision making. While you cannot always guarantee the best outcome, you can be confident that you took the time to make a proper assessment before making a decision.

To better frame your determination, asking yourself these questions will help. Is this important or not? Could a wrong decision harm an individual or the business? Will I be able to take corrective action if needed? What is the size of the potential impact?

Let us look at this through the eyes of a child. My daughter did not enjoy going into the candy store as a young girl. Not because she did not love candy, but because her mother and I told her she could only buy one thing. She was quickly overwhelmed by the expectation and unable to make a decision, often walking out of the store with no candy. As people in everyday situations, we can be a lot like my daughter in a candy store stressed about making a wrong decision and not wanting to commit. We limit our ability to move forward by getting stuck in analysis paralysis, where you become paralyzed in deciding due to over analyzing.

It can be helpful to stop to assess the potential impact of a decision. Suppose the difference between option A and option B will have minimal impact. In that case, you can be confident in making an immediate decision as there will not be a significant difference in the outcome. Other times you can be satisfied if you know a decision can be changed later. Hence, getting an answer right the first time may not be crucial.

You could apply this principle to target shooting. Someone can aim three times and then fire, trying to hit the bullseye. Or they could aim, shoot, adjust, shoot, adjust, shoot. The second approach will get quicker and better results. The quick decision to repeatedly narrow your focus increases the probability of success. Active modification can help reach a goal more effectively than continually working to find one "perfect" answer.

You can even implement this decision-making technique for simple tasks such as email. When possible, respond to emails as they are received. It takes twice as long to put off the response than to take care of it the first time. You may end up rereading an email multiple times if you delay responding. This can result in continually returning to the email because of an unwillingness to commit to a decision. Remember, while more time to consider can be good in some cases, it is only sometimes beneficial.

This decision-making process supports the "only touch things once" principle commonly recommended by efficiency gurus. The idea changes slightly if I need more information, but the conscious effort remains the same. If not intentional, your behaviors and responses become merely a pattern, not a purposeful decision-making process.

Once you practice asking whether more information is needed, it will begin to happen naturally, influencing even the moments with limited decision-making time. You will more clearly notice when a decision needs to be made immediately and when it does not. Struggling to decide on something may indicate that it is not yet time to determine an answer or it is not necessary for one to be made. Thinking through all aspects of every decision may appear daunting to some. Still it is a process everyone can benefit from and can become habitual, requiring little effort.

Teams can significantly benefit from this decision-making mindset. I have sat in business meetings where members left the meeting with no clear plan because they had spent the entire time debating outcomes. Without creating a definitive plan for reaching a goal, meetings lose their value. You may find Chapter 15, "You Must Have Great Meetings," helpful. When the team is trying to make a decision, team members sometimes offer input that does not impact the decision. By focusing only on what information is impactful, teams can reach an answer faster and make better decisions.

Think of this principle like an SAT math word problem where you are asked to read the information provided to solve a question. Some context is necessary to determine the answer, while the rest may be superfluous. Because you cannot find additional outside information when taking the SAT exam, you must adopt an immediate decision-making strategy and use only what information is provided to decide on an answer.

While in a team meeting, if the missing information can be easily discovered with a phone call, doing so could expedite the decision-making process and potentially conclude the meeting or generate the next discussion topic. If more information is not readily available, it may require additional time and research. Before the session ends you should establish an action plan assigning who is responsible for gathering needed facts. Once the new information is obtained, the entire group may not need to reconvene. One individual or a few members may be sufficient to move forward and reach a now obvious decision based on the new information.

The team may also be able to pre-determine an answer based on anticipated new information such as option A is the choice if the new information is "x" and option B if the new data is "y." Alternatively, the group may agree to defer the decision to a single person whom they trust will know the best solution once "x" and "y" are discerned.

To facilitate this decision-making process, I sometimes do not answer people immediately when they ask me a question. Instead, I pause and mentally consider the potential answers. I need a few seconds to contemplate. If I realize it is not something I need to find more information on, I will provide an answer. This often helps me make decisions faster and with more confidence.

It is crucial to recognize how different personality types influence the decision-making process. For example, extroverted personalities, those who think by talking things out may find this momentary pre-decision pondering difficult. Some people cannot settle on a next step until they have verbally worked through all the relevant possibilities. Their role in the decision-making process is to talk through all aspects of the topic and bring them to the table. If you identify as someone who is explorative and dissatisfied with limited options, you may be an ISFP on the Myers-Briggs 16 personalities test. [2] A decision-making strategy can help ISFPs work through their natural tendencies to reach an answer and accept a team's decision more comfortably.

A second example is that people who love to learn prefer to avoid moving forward with a decision because they enjoy exploring all the options. Additionally, some people find satisfaction in reaching a definitive conclusion while others do so through information discovery. My wife enjoys exploring options. If we are planning a vacation, she loves looking at 20 different resorts and deciding which one is best based on reviews and pictures. Conversely, this can feel exhausting for those

---

2 "Adventurer Personality." 16 Personalities https://www.16personalities.com/isfp-personality.

who want to pick a resort and go. But for Julie, part of the joy of vacationing is seeing the options beforehand, reviewing what every place has to offer, and picturing herself there before ultimately booking the trip.

Therefore, when confronted with a decision, consider the consequences of every potential answer and ask yourself whether more information is needed. If there is a limited negative impact for all possible answers, feel free to make a decision and readjust later if needed. However, if more information is required, determine what it is and who is needed to help make that decision. Doing this will make decisions quicker, achieve better results, and reduce stress.

CHALLENGE

Before making your next decision, consider if more information will alter your choice. If you already have all the facts, avoid wasting time revisiting the topic again later by making a decision now. If not, determine what information you need and how you are going to get it.

15

3

QUANTITATIVE DECISION MAKING

When do I use quantitative decision making?

Do not ask what the answer is, ask what it is not.

Deciding on an answer can be hard when there is a range of possibilities. It is even harder when there is limited information to help reveal the best choice. I find it beneficial to start by determining the lowest and highest possible quantity. This narrows the potential values and allows a decision to be made quicker with a higher level of confidence.

"Quantitative decision-making methods can be used when:

1. There is a clearly stated objective.

2. There are several alternative courses of action.

3. There is a calculable measure of the benefit or worth of the various alternatives." [3]

If you are a parent, you may already be familiar with this strategy and not even know it. When deciding on the right bedtime for your kids, you may have used quantitative

---

3 Levin, Richard. I., 1984, "Statistics for Management," Prentice-Hall, New Jersey. (Prentice-Hall International Series in Management)

decision making to assist you. By considering the child's age and the earliest and latest time you would allow them to be in bed, you referenced this range and narrowed it to the best possible bedtime.

While children's nighttime routines may not be the normal subject matter at the office, this same decision-making technique is quite valuable in a business setting. For example, let us imagine your company is considering a price hike and you are trying to figure out the best percentage to increase. Without a range from which to base your decision-making process, it can be difficult to pick the best percent. But if the team collectively determines 5% is the absolute highest price increase the company would consider, then you have begun to establish parameters for your decision greater than 0% and less than 5%. As you continue to quantitatively narrow the options, you may come to realize a 1% rate hike would not justify all the communication efforts and emotions normally associated with a price increase. So 2.5% becomes the new lowest potential percentage increase. Thus the increase will be no less than 2.5% and no greater than 5%.

This range offers a more definitive way to come to a decision when too many options make the decision difficult. You can more effectively land on a final answer by whittling down from the highest and lowest outlying options and considering the consequences in between. What is the trade-off of risk versus reward between 5% and 4%? Is the 1% difference significant enough to lose customers? If so, then it is probably not worth a 5% increase instead of 4%, and you have just successfully narrowed your potential price increase range even further, no less than 2.5% and no greater than 4%.

Now what about choosing 3%? But is the extra half percentage point versus 2.5% worth the risk? If the answer is "yes" and it is believed that customers will not be lost at 3% over 2.5%, then your decision is now somewhere between a 3% and 4% price increase.

At this point you have taken the decision-making process from any possible answer to somewhere between 3% and 4%. This is now a much easier decision to make as well as to achieve team consensus. You may say, "Look, if we're going to go through with the effort of instituting a price increase, we might as well go for the 4% especially since customers will probably react the same whether it is 3% or 4%."

At that moment, you have successfully decided on a 4% price increase through quantitative decision making. In the process, you narrowed your margin of error down to 1%. You started with a blank piece of paper and zero idea on what percent to increase the price. This process of eliminating poorer choices helps lead to the answer with the highest probability of success. Additionally, your margin of error is significantly smaller because you have analyzed the outer options of the possibility range and assessed the risk and reward. It is easier to start this way, by whittling your potential answers down, rather than trying to pick an acceptable number.

Quantitative decision making helps reach a consensus more quickly and effectively among a team. Collectively agreeing early in the process that the company would never go above a 5% price increase helps you all work within the 2.5% to 5% range. The team immediately has greater clarity on what kind of input to contribute and can do so confidently because of the numerical parameters. Valuable discussion prompts an educated decision in less time than if quantitative strategies had not been utilized.

Be cautious to not just pick the middle of your range. If you have 2.5% and 5% as your outer limits, do not simply say, "Let's split the difference." I find that is rarely the best answer. There is not much logic to simply choosing the middle when there is obvious motivation to either land at the top or bottom of your range.

Perhaps the only time you may split the difference is if you are unsure whether to go through with a 2.5% or 5% increase. Maybe you believe the risk–reward of 2.5% increase is equivalent to the risk–reward of 5% and you cannot come up with a definitive answer. But equal probability of success does not mean the risk versus reward is equivalent. A 2.5% increase is a much smaller reward with potentially lower risk compared to a 5% increase with both a larger reward and risk.

The point here is you rarely know for sure. In our example, will the 5% increase cost you more customers than the revenue the increase generates? Is it safer to promote the 2.5% increase instead and keep more customers but at a comparatively lower revenue? If you initially had quantitative numbers for each of these scenarios, and they essentially came out to the same revenue projection, then you may have a difficult time deciding whether to lean more toward the lower or upper end of that range, and thus may choose the middle.

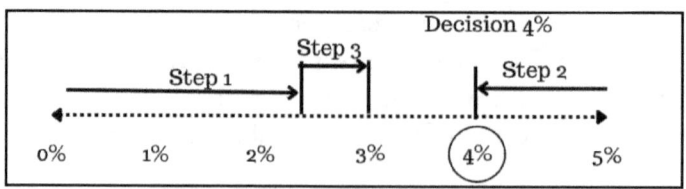

Chapter 2, "Timing of Decision Making" can be another valuable tool in this process. There, I challenge you to evaluate whether you need to become smarter before making a decision. This means deciding if additional information or more time for contemplation is needed to increase the odds of a better decision. Utilizing this "smarter" principle as you narrow your answer from the highest and lowest values on your quantitative range means regularly asking yourself, "Do I need to become smarter to pick a final answer?" If you are considering a 2.5% to 5% price increase, maybe it would be beneficial to talk to someone else for input before deciding on the possible range of answers or the final answer. You also might want to research what the competition is doing, what other employees think, or talk to a few of your best customers to get a better sense for the potential impact of your decision. At some point you will conclude you are not going to become smarter by getting more information and must simply make a decision with the information at hand.

There are many quantitative decisions to be made. How many marketing dollars should be spent? How many people should be hired? What is the budget for a specific project? What is the timeline allowed for the completion of a task? How much inventory should be carried? What should be the payment terms? How many customers can a salesperson support? What new territories should be expanded? What is the anticipated ROI (return on investment)? There are also related questions for non-profit organizations, like: How many fundraising events do we want? How many sponsors should we have for each event?

As part of your due diligence when deciding between the highest and lowest set points, pause and ask the team, "While we think we are right about our assumptions, what happens if we are wrong?" Chapter 23, "Think Right, Assume Wrong" provides insight into an attitude that can help lead you to the best answer and avoid pitfalls. Seeking out more information to secure a greater level of confidence in your decision through further research or additional input brings this quantitative methodology full circle.

This process is not only meant for decisions with a numerical range, as virtually any selection of options can be quantitatively evaluated. By using this process, you will be amazed at how much quicker you come to decisions. You will also become more confident in your answers. The team will understand the assumptions used to get to the decision. Consensus will be easier to achieve. So do not start with asking what is the answer; start with what the answer should not be, by first identifying the highest and lowest possible answers.

CHALLENGE

Would using this approach have changed the answer the last time a decision was needed?

Is there currently a decision you or the team needs to make that can utilize this process?

4

When to Hit the Panic Button

Know when immediate action is necessary.

When is worrying positive and when is it negative?

Realize how your reactions affect others.

Stress can be positive or negative. It can be a motivation to take action or debilitating. Great leaders know when to worry, when to take immediate action, and when not to create alarm. Too often, leaders get stressed when they do not need to or it is not time yet. A leader may need to develop a sense of urgency to elicit prompt action. Determining when it is appropriate to develop such urgency is an integral part of leadership.

Consider the potential negative impact on yourself and others if you panic. Is the issue short-term or long-term? What is the magnitude of potential harm? Do you have all the facts? Leaders who know the appropriate response can have two significantly positive impacts. First, they will be better decision-makers and be ahead of the competition in problem solving. Second, those within their organization will experience less stress and know how to navigate issues better because of the leader's example.

This chapter is not a guide on how to react to panic or manage stress. It is also not about how to move forward in a situation to resolve a problem. There are plenty of books already on shelves about those topics. Instead, the goal of this chapter focuses on helping leaders acknowledge initial thoughts when presented with unexpected situations, then accurately assess and ask, "Should I hit the panic button or not?"

Often, there is not enough information to know how or whether to react. As a result, we resort to worrying and reacting emotionally rather than assessing a situation. A classic example of a healthy panic response is if you are walking in the woods and a bear appears before you, then you must act immediately. When faced with a situation that causes concern, we need to always assess how to react. Is it a time to panic, or will there be time to resolve or acquire information before deciding?

In Harper Lee's *To Kill a Mockingbird*, Atticus reminds Scout, "It's not time to worry yet." This quote implies there is not cause for immediate reaction. The part I like most about this quote is including the final word "yet." It suggests there will be times when you need to worry and gather more information. There can be instances when worrying is appropriate, forcing you to take immediate action. But it would be best not to always have your hand hovering over the panic button.

Mark Twain once said, "I am an old man and have known a great many troubles, but most of them never happened."[4]

---

4 Attributed to Mark Twain in *Reader's Digest*, Apr. 1934.

People spend too much time worrying about the unknown and what-ifs, time they will not get back, only to find those concerns never actually occur.

Often in business, people panic, which is not beneficial. Therefore, leaders must demonstrate reasonable and controlled behavior when others get flustered. However, suppose a customer is experiencing a quality issue posing a potential threat of a significant financial loss. In that case, it is appropriate to act quickly and institute an all-hands-on-deck approach to resolve the problem.

A typical situation where leaders need help deciding when to worry or not is if a customer makes a demand or threatens to leave. Leaders must quickly assess the moment rather than panic. Suppose the customer represents a large percentage of total revenue and can indeed switch easily to a competitor. In that case, it may be time to panic and take immediate action.

When a competitor steals a customer, panic often arises within an organization. Sometimes it is unnecessary until you get more information to determine if that customer is truly lost. The concern may result from an inaccurate rumor, or you may decide you are better off without the customer. I have seen many situations where a business lost a customer and became more successful because it began focusing on more profitable customers. Sometimes a customer might leave a company only to quickly return and grow their loyalty after realizing the grass is not greener on the other side. So when faced with a significant customer issue, do not immediately overreact, which can cause short and long-term harm.

When I receive calls from panicked employees worried about something that has gone wrong, I try always to respond calmly and assess the situation with them. Even if my heart is saying, "Oh no, this is terrible," I remind myself that may not be true. If you maintain a composed demeanor, it helps others to relax and better focus on the issue at hand. Their initial panic is something I appreciate because it shows they care. On the other hand, if I were to brush off every problem in front of me and say, "We will figure it out," their panic and the situation could worsen. The employee may stop bringing up urgent issues. Employees will not always have all the information needed to assess a situation properly on their own. They rely on their leader's knowledge and experience to accurately determine a situation's severity. I like to remind employees that if everything went smoothly all the time, many of our jobs would not be needed, which is also highlighted in Chapter 10, "Complexity May Be Good."

Adopting a proactive approach to panic is not exclusive to business. I believe decisions related to one's health to be the most challenging. When experiencing an unusual ache or pain, it is natural to feel concerned about what medical test results might reveal. However, I tell my wife there is no value in worrying about a future test result. Science has proved worrying can physically harm your body. Therefore, it is not time to worry if worrying does not add value to a situation.

Emotional individuals may find this concept difficult and even uncomfortable. That is okay. When you go through an assessment of a situation, you still may not be able to stop yourself from worrying. For example, if you are concerned about something like a medical test, but realize there is nothing you can do about it right now, you have made a healthy evaluation. Sometimes reminding yourself, "There is nothing I can do about this now," can be the key to proper assessment. It will help you navigate those times when you need to wait for an answer to know whether something negative will come to fruition. Conversely, I know people who have had health issues but chose not to worry about the symptoms they were experiencing... so the situation worsened because they did not take action soon enough. This chapter is not about the good or bad of panicking; it is about making a conscious decision on when immediate action is necessary and when not to panic.

People are made up of all different types of personalities. Those who approach decision making from a hard facts perspective may process a situation differently than those with a higher emphasis on emotions. However, successful leadership requires an awareness that both responses can be beneficial, depending on the situation. In the book *Leading with Feeling*, the authors interviewed 25 mid-level and senior-level leaders of various organizations and asked them to describe incidents where they had "managed or used emotion ... to deal with a problem or achieve a goal." The consensus was clear from an engineering firm going through the Great Recession of 2008 to an HR department feeling heavy internal performance pressure. "Leaders ultimately succeed or fail based on how much good information they have ... [and] much of the information we communicate ... is done through our emotions. [Therefore] monitoring the emotional climate ... is a savvy strategy for any leader." [5]

Great leaders know what is essential in their lives and use those values and priorities to determine when to react immediately. What is important to you? Is it health, money, employees, or customers? Whatever you define as

---

5 Excerpt from *Leading with Feeling*, published in Fast Company.

important is going to drive your decision making. If it is money, you will decide how to react based on the monetary impact. If it is health, you will react based on how to avoid stress. Do not be quick to label all aspects of your life as equally important, but use what is essential to guide your decisions on when to panic and when not to panic.

CHALLENGE

The next time you feel yourself panicking, stop and determine if an immediate action is needed. If you have time to address the situation there is no need to panic.

Popular Books Related to This Topic:

Why Zebras Don't Get Ulcers by Robert M. Sapolsky

Managing the Unexpected by Kathleen Sutcliffe

Great at Work by Morten T. Hansen

The Making of a Manager by Julie Zhou

5
E.A.S.E.

Ease stands for:

Eliminate
Automate
Simplify
Enhance

I came up with this acronym early in my career. Too many reports were being created, and employees were spending too much time on non-value added tasks. As I was haphazardly trying to improve the situation, over time, I realized there are four specific steps in the sequence needed to improve operations systematically. So I developed the saying, "Tasks and reports should be evaluated for E.A.S.E."

First, determine if a task, report, or even a meeting can be eliminated. Suppose no action is being taken as a result of the report or meeting. In that case, it should be eliminated because it is does not add value. By stopping, you can replace the time with more value-added tasks.

Sometimes you can test whether a task or report adds value by simply stopping it. Does anyone notice? Is there an impact on the business? Also consider eliminating tasks or reports that do not add value to your customers. Sometimes we continue providing customer reports and information after it is no longer needed.

Second, if a task, report, or meeting cannot be eliminated, determine if it can be automated to reduce the human effort. For example, can a report be automatically generated. Can you automate customer communications such as order taking, acknowledgment, shipping confirmation, and change request notices? Could any of these be automated? Any automation will allow you to spend more time and energy on tasks that should or must involve humans.

Third, to simplify a task or report, consider what steps or data can be removed without impacting the business or customer. Simplifying makes everything take less time and become less complex. If the task is difficult, it takes a more experienced or skilled employee. If it can be simplified, it can be done by a less experienced employee.

Simplification is not only about conserving time but also focus. When reports round off dollars to the nearest hundred or thousand, it can help people concentrate more clearly on the bigger picture. Or looking only at a top 10 list rather than showing every number also keeps the focus on where it is most important. Using LEAN process improvement can be a good systematic approach to simplification. LEAN focuses on the activities which create value.

Fourth, consider if items can be enhanced. Maybe a report, task, or meeting does not need to be eliminated, automated, or simplified. It may need to include better information. Perhaps it could provide more or better data, be timelier, or add more value. E.A.S.E. is not just about minimizing but also adding the most value with the available resources. What tasks, reports, meetings, and actions could be enhanced and leveraged to offer better outcomes?

Some examples of where E.A.S.E. can impact a business:

ANNUAL REVIEWS

I have made E.A.S.E. a part of the employee annual review process. Accountability reports can be automatically generated so employees understand where their performance falls before review time. In addition, I request that some employees come to the annual review with tangible examples of where they applied E.A.S.E., letting me know exactly what they eliminated, automated, simplified, or enhanced.

Or maybe the annual review form(s) could be simplified into a format that requires less input. Also consider whether the process might be enhanced by including something new, such as evaluating how the company is performing against its mission statement.

In most positions in a growing company, I estimate employees are required to complete 20% more tasks every three years. Without applying E.A.S.E. or delegating, after three years, they are going to have to be doing 120% of their current workload. My goal for incorporating E.A.S.E. in this situation is that 20% of the existing effort must be eliminated, automated, simplified, or enhanced every three years, allowing employees to stay at 100% capacity.

REPORTS AND MEETINGS

Consider whether somebody can be eliminated from a meeting, task participation, or report distribution. Maybe only invite employees to meetings if they can impact discussions or will be impacted. Perhaps report distribution can be automated to eliminate manual effort. Processes which contain multiple tasks may be an excellent place to start evaluating for E.A.S.E.

Budget Building

Budget building is a process that could benefit from E.A.S.E. because it occurs annually. Are there budget reports that could be eliminated because that level of detail is no longer required? Could the reports be simplified to provide more actionable detail? Are there people who could be eliminated from the budget-building process?

Can any parts of the budgeting process be automated by generating drafts from prior year data, or three-year averages? For example, can low-dollar or non-variable budget items be simplified using a default formula or logic-driven equation?

Are there enhanced ways to look at previous sales information to better understand where new sales will come from, or where the potential to lose sales exists? Too often the budget-building process spends too much time looking at expenses rather than analyzing sales.

Inventory

Are there steps in the inventory process that could be eliminated, such as cycle counts? If history shows there are little or no deviations, then stop doing cycle counts if they are not worth the time that goes into them.

Another possibility for elimination is the effort to place material orders. If traditionally, all inventory is ordered at the same frequency, once per month, then why not order three months' worth to reduce the number of orders to process, receive, stock, match to a purchase order, and pay?

Is there anything that could be automated within the inventory process? Exception reporting can, perhaps quarterly, alert designated team members to fast or slow-moving inventory based on agreed-upon definitions.

Can tasks like handling and sorting, labeling, shipping, or inventory storage be simplified? An enhancement might be adding SKUs to inventory or ensure parts reach customers in a timely manner.

CUSTOMER COMMUNICATIONS

Is there anything currently being communicated to customers that they do not value? Can such communication be eliminated? Can any customer communication be automated without losing personal connection? Reports with 10 things can be simplified to two, or only feature highlights rather than details. Is it helpful to enhance current communication in some way? For example, perhaps an email to customers when their product is shipped would be a differentiation from your competitors. It may be helpful to add the Purchase Order inside an email, include tracking information, or provide a link to the online manual for a product being shipped.

MARKETING

An ever-important question is whether some marketing should be eliminated because it has been quantifiably shown to generate less sales than the effort or expense required. With the rise in remote work, additional marketing may need to pivot or adapt to new technologies to reach targeted audiences more successfully. Sending physical marketing pieces to an office may be fruitless because employees are no longer there.

How can automation be used? Whole automated marketing software packages have been created so particular customer actions trigger automatic follow-ups. For example, based

33

on customer and prospect behavior, if they click a certain link on your website, it can automatically send them an email or alert your sales rep. If they spend so many minutes or visit a certain page, a pop-up can prompt them to opt-in for more information or to schedule a call with a sales rep.

Marketing automation can analyze buying behavior. For example, suppose you purchase a particular item on Amazon. In that case, the site suggests you may also be interested in additional related items which are often purchased together.

Simplify marketing to only focus on specific target markets rather than a broad industry. You also might outsource tasks such as stuffing and sorting bulk mailings. Another possibility is to simplify a website, removing layers of information that have been added over the years. Often a stripped-down, more simplistic website conveys a product or service stronger.

To enhance, begin by analyzing which marketing drives value that justifies its expense, then enhance those elements. Focus on what your customers most want. Can you provide them with product reviews or video tutorials?

Accounting

Accounting processes are often ripe for evaluation using E.A.S.E. Many practices continue solely because they have been done for a long time. Examine which can quickly be eliminated. Can some reports be simplified? For example, it is standard practice to prepare financials every month, but many companies take no action whatsoever based on them. If so, why not only prepare financials quarterly? Can exception reports be automated for accounting activities, so they do not have to be manually created? Or can current reports be enhanced to highlight or focus only on actionable information for managers?

HR

Examine your Human Resources processes. Are there reports or activities that could be eliminated? Are there elements like forms that might be automated or performed online rather than by hand? Can some of the forms be simplified to include only the information needed? Would a checklist allow new hires to know better what to expect? Perhaps HR can find ways to enhance employee work-life balance, making it more enjoyable and fulfilling.

PRODUCT RETURNS

What can be done to eliminate product returns? Could you include more detailed product descriptions, reviews, or images on the website? Can the return process be automated, auto-generating shipping labels that are scannable by your receiving department? Can returns be simplified by asking for less information or eliminating steps that slow down the process? Can they be enhanced by asking for specific feedback so appropriate action can be taken to reduce returns?

CHALLENGE

Track specific ways you implement E.A.S.E. over the next month to see how many improvements you can make.

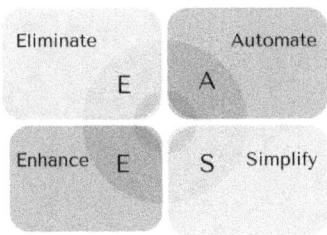

6

ACTIONABLE INFO

Discover the litmus test for evaluating data.

**Increase efficiency by determining
which reports are necessary.**

Businesses need to be run using what I call "actionable information." Each day you are likely inundated with information, however, actionable information only exists if you are willing and able to take action when data indicates change is needed.

The difference between actionable information and key performance indicators (KPIs) is that KPIs often generate lots of data, tracking whether that data is above or below KPI. Still, they do not necessarily create an action, especially not in real-time. Therefore, identifying KPIs is important, but you must take the additional step to determine what is needed to be reported immediately when an exception occurs to a KPI.

Here is a litmus test to reference when evaluating if the information is actionable:

- If the data trends up or down, is there an action taken?

- If the reported trend is desired, what action provoked the change to sustain it?

- If the trend is undesired, what corrective action can be implemented to change the trajectory back to where it needs to be?

Patterns that are reflected by data in your critical measures of success are not meant to simply keep score; they should be actionable.

Many businesses focus on KPIs, but often fall short of identifying actions needed for improvement. Success is not about having data; it is about having data that allows a business to respond effectively to negative situations and take the best advantage of positive ones. Operational data collection is valuable, but only when you understand what to pay attention to. Otherwise, you may fall victim to information overload and analysis paralysis.

With the advent of computers and ever-increasing processing speeds and capacity, the ability to capture, store and present data has grown. As a result, the term "big data" [6,7] has been in use since the 1990s and refers to complex data sets that are difficult for your current software to capture, curate, manage, and process within a tolerable time frame. [8]

---

6 John R. Mashey (25 April 1998). "Big Data ... and the Next Wave of InfraStress" (PDF). Slides from invited talk. Usenix. Retrieved 28 September 2016.

7 Steve Lohr (1 February 2013). "The Origins of 'Big Data': An Etymological Detective Story." *The New York Times.* Retrieved 28 September 2016.

8 Snijders, C.; Matzat, U.; and Reips, U.-D. (2012). "'Big Data': Big gaps of knowledge in the field of Internet." *International Journal of Internet Science* 7:1–5.

While big data likely fuels some of your reporting, for it to be helpful, it must produce actionable information through real-time exception reporting. Exception reporting highlights the data that deviates significantly from expectations and flags it for your attention. If there is an exceptionally high or low item in the data, only that anomaly should be reported. All surrounding information that falls within expectations should not be reported, only the exception is communicated. This way, everyone can know what needs to be done without becoming overwhelmed by information.

After reading Chapter 5, E.A.S.E., you can see how this can be applied to actionable information.

Too Detailed   Better, but no call to action   Identifies exceptions only

- Eliminate entire reports or parts if they do not produce actionable information and are not legally required.

- Automate reporting to show only exceptions.

- Simplify information to focus on what is actionable and only send it to those in a position to take action. The importance of simplification is to remove any unnecessary data or steps, so the process is less time-consuming for all involved. Suppose something is no longer needed or has little or no impact on the business or customer. In that case, it can be eliminated, allowing everyone to be able to focus on only those things that are important... those that will generate actionable information.

- Enhance reporting by determining if additional information could be provided to generate beneficial actions.

ACTIONABLE INFORMATION BY DEPARTMENT:

Sales

Before you can use actionable information reporting, you first need to decide how to track your sales department. There are two options:

1. Measuring results: How many sales were achieved in a week?

2. Measuring behavior: How many calls were made in a week?

Deciding which one to track will depend on the type of business and the personalities of the sales representatives. Measuring behaviors can be best if the sales representative has limited impact on financial results. Measuring results is better if the quantity of activities is less important than completing a sale.

Actionable information based on measuring behaviors would occur by determining how many calls should be made and creating an exception report when that number has not been reached or was exceeded. For example, if the goal was 50 calls a week, then an exception report can go to the manager if there were only 30 calls made so that it can be learned why the goal was not met. If instead, there were 70 calls made, the manager can congratulate and encourage the sales rep to keep up the great work. The concept is that no action will occur if there are 31-69 calls, so no need to send a report.

Actionable information based on measuring results can be actual versus budgeted quantity or dollar amount of weekly sales, then creating an exception report only when sales are above or below 10 percent of budget. If the sales rep exceeds that figure, the message goes out, and the person can be congratulated. If they fall below, you can check to see what resources are needed to catch up.

Another results based report a sales manager might watch is "days invoice not paid," with an exception report being generated if an invoice goes beyond a fixed number of days. When an exception report is triggered, someone can follow up with those involved in the sale to determine why the customer has not paid promptly.

It is imperative that if you manage based on actionable information and exception reporting, someone must pay close attention to all reports that are generated. There will be fewer reports, but each will contain critical information. If every report identifies actionable information, then every report needs to be reviewed and appropriate action taken. If someone misses even one report in this circumstance, somebody will miss a corresponding action. To often businesses generate so many reports that they get ignored, or there is too much data and the salient information is missed.

Finance

There are three buckets of financial reporting: sales, margin, and overhead.

- For sales, daily or weekly reports provide the top line, as mentioned earlier.

- For margin, use exception reporting for margins by product, service, or customer.

- For overhead (Sales, General, & Administrative expenses), this can be managed based on approval for each expenditure, without much concern whether the total costs are up or down. If every expense is being justified and approved, the total expense for the month does not really matter since every expenditure has been approved proactively, based on actionable information.

You can now have managers focus on real-time, day-to-day operations because they are no longer inundated with excess data reports. However, just because they can redirect their time does not mean their new responsibilities will not lead to more data generation elsewhere, not to mention that "the average company loses about $15 million each year due to poor data quality." [9]

One industry that uses exception reporting incredibly well is credit card companies. Their algorithms are so sophisticated that when there is any abnormal change in card usage, they identify in real-time and immediately alert the customer of the potential fraud. It can be as simple as a few dollars spent in a store not normally visited or a sequence of transactions within a short time frame. Their algorithm renders exceptions the moment they occur, and a phone call confirms whether the transaction is legitimate.

---

9 Operational Exception Reporting in EBS: Exploring a Better Way—insightsoftware

All businesses can financially benefit from implementing this kind of actionable exception reporting.

Expense management

If expenses are not managed and approved individually, then a budgeted amount is created. No action is needed as long as costs stay within that budgeted amount. Exception reporting identifies only expenses that exceed that budget. For example, the U.S. government approves an annual fixed-budget amount. They utilize exception reporting by focusing only when projected expenses are over budget.

Marketing

While it is difficult to track precise Return on Investment (ROI) for marketing initiatives, prospects' behaviors can still be measured.

You may not be able to ascertain whether a Google pay-per-click ad generated a sale, or if other factors influenced the sale, however, you could track behaviors the ad generated, such as the number of clicks or calls. In marketing, this provides actionable information that allows decisions to be made based on what behaviors occurred and how it would be best to utilize that data for future marketing initiatives and spending.

With email, perhaps your next newsletter is set to hit 1,000 in-boxes by the end of the week. You have included some essential news about the business. Your marketing team came to work the following Monday to report that only 200 emails were actually opened.

What happened?

This scenario is a classic reality when sending an eblast to prospects and customers. This business believed it was sending out 1,000 monthly or quarterly newsletters when on average 80% of its prospects never actually engaged with the information. An actionable piece of information may be to monitor the email opens and mail a physical copy to the 800 who did not open the email.

Production

Production exception reporting is one of the biggest areas that can benefit from actionable information. The key is to simplify and reduce the number of reports provided. There is often a plethora of reports about how many units were produced based on:

- The speed of the line

- Shift performance

- Number and reason for product returns

These reports are informative, yet far too often, no action is taken. Every production report ought to be looked at for a possible action. If that presents difficulty, what type of new report would be more beneficial?

For example, if machine downtime is higher than usual, then immediate action needs to be taken to increase preventative maintenance. If production is not meeting the units required, you may need to notify customers of potential delays. These are examples of actionable information that make daily reporting worthwhile. Reports that merely show what has been produced that day do not offer actionable information.

Human Resources

Suppose performance reviews include measurable results for the year. In that case, actionable information and exception reporting can identify employees with goals that they are not on track to achieve. Once identified, HR can implement regular reporting that measures progress toward these goals rather than waiting for a performance review at the end of the year—with no time to adjust behaviors. At year end, there is not much action that can be taken other than to plan differently for the next year.

Non-profits

Non-profits cannot measure results based on profits. This creates a challenge that sometimes causes non-profits to just focus on promoting the intangible benefits of their services. Instead, they may find it beneficial to identify specific actionable information that will generate the best actions to achieve their mission. While a result may be challenging to objectively measure for non-profits, they can measure the level of beneficial actions completed.

Internal Fraud

It only takes a few specific exception reports to stop the makings of fraudulent activity by employees before it ever evolves into a major crime. According to the International Monetary Fund, internal theft represents approximately 5% of all lost business revenue annually. [10]

---

10 Susan Moore. "How to Stop Data Quality Undermining Your Business." *Gartner*, Jan. 28, 2018. https://www.gartner.com/smarterwithgartner/how-to-stop-data-quality-undermining-your-business

Exception reporting brings to the surface the data and behaviors that are out of the ordinary, not only to examine what is going well and what may need redirection but also to detect patterns that signal theft. When key measurables and actionable information are not being tracked and acted upon, fraudulent activity can go a long time without being discovered. For example, the Association of Certified Fraud Examiners notes that a "typical employee theft scheme lasts 14 months before it is detected." [11]

TIME TO STOP SENDING NON-ACTIONABLE INFORMATION

If it's difficult to assess whether a report is actionable and needed, one test is to stop sending the report and see if anyone notices. I once worked where many reports were sent out daily, weekly, and monthly. Gradually I stopped sending one report at a time. Many times no one noticed the reports were no longer being sent.

Verdict: Those reports were not presenting actionable information.

The most common business report is the monthly financial statement. Does it present actionable information? Many businesses do not take monthly action if results go up or down. Compounding the issue is that these statements are distributed weeks after the performance occurred.

Many businesses would be better off only generating financial reports quarterly. They should rely on implementing exception reporting on actionable

---

11 Milica Milenkovic. "30+ Surprising Employee Theft Statistics and Facts" (2022 Edition). *Small Biz Genius*. Mar. 25, 2022. https://www.smallbizgenius. net/by-the-numbers/employee-theft-statistics/#gref

information throughout the month (daily or weekly) that identifies when something needs to be addressed that impacts financials. Most of the Peak Capital businesses only produce financial statements quarterly. We do not manage by these statements, we pay attention to our daily and weekly metrics.

A report showing margin by product and margin by customer will highlight much more actionable information than just a consolidated financial statement. The goal is that as you pay more attention to daily and weekly reports and not after-the-fact financial statements, you will already know what the monthly results will be by the time financials are generated.

But reports are not the only time-thieves in business. I once had a boss who wanted confirmation when somebody completed every request he made. I have adopted the opposite approach in my business based on exception reporting. I only want to be notified when something has yet to be done by the agreed deadline. For example, if I request something from you and we agree that it is going to be done by next Wednesday, I do not need to know it was done on-time. If the timeline changes, such as an earlier completion date, or an anticipated delay, then you can let me know. Otherwise, if it is done by Wednesday, I do not need the additional confirmation. The more reporting and feedback elimination that can be adopted, the easier it is to build efficiency by only receiving and focusing on actionable information.

CHALLENGE

Whenever you receive a report this week, decide if it causes you to take action.

7

Focus Days

Focus days can be essential to achieving long-term goals.

What makes a successful focus day?

It is incredibly beneficial to block off an entire day for a focus day, not necessarily to relax the mind, but rather for strategic thinking. One of the things lost in business today is the discipline of thinking about life goals and what behaviors are needed to reach them. For me, a focus day is not dedicated solely to creativity or a single project, although both can be beneficial. Instead, it is a conscious effort to take a step back, view my goals with a long-term perspective, and consider what I need to do to accomplish them.

A focus session generally consists of:

1. clearing the mind

2. reviewing and reflecting on notes of previous sessions

3. selecting topics of importance for the session

4. spending time focusing on topics with no distractions

5. documenting thoughts and action items

I like to set the tone of a focus day from the beginning with something relaxing and mind-clearing, like reading a book or getting a massage. The key is to remove all distractions throughout the day. No phone, no email, and nothing else should take your focus off what is important. If that is not possible for the entire day, block off one or two 15-minute intervals to check your email or attend to necessities. However, the risk of viewing even a single email or answering a phone message is the emotional response created that distracts you from your focus day. Even after reading an email, you may continue to think about it.

Once I have spent time clearing my thoughts, I look at the notes from my last focus day. This action establishes accountability and puts me in the right frame of mind. As I look at the ideas generated before, I evaluate how they were brought about and assess what has been done in response. If something is incomplete, I determine whether that should become a part of this day's focus.

The next part of the agenda is to select topics you want to consider for the rest of the day. These can be work-related or personal development opportunities. It is important to take notes throughout the day because you will find your mind easily wanders. Note-taking will allow you to capture everything generated during the day and specific actions you want to take.

Note-taking is also beneficial when a distracting reminder pops up about something you need to do tomorrow. You can write it down, forget about it, and continue on with your focus day, knowing you can reference your notes at a later time. I try to avoid using a computer during my focus days because it can become a distraction difficult to avoid. If, for some reason, you need to use a computer, then be sure to turn off all notifications, close your email app, and do not access social media.

Regarding topics and ideas generated, I like to leave the focus day with written action items. I do not want to spend the time just thinking about theories with no concrete responses. I also do not want a two-page project plan either. When I find myself beginning to create more specific steps, I must stop and remind myself that I will take care of the details later. I can use the time now to explore other topics or think about more long-term goals.

Topics can include anything relevant to your life. It can be about how to become a better spouse or parent. Or consider how you expect to achieve career goals, more importantly, clarifying what are and are not your career goals. What significant projects should you be pursuing on the job? How could a team work more effectively as a result? How do you want to change your perspective on life? Whatever your goals, you should come away from your focus day with specific actions to complete and finalized decisions.

FOCUS
Day Set-up

- Schedule Day
- Pick Location
- Remove Distractions
- Review notes from last focus day
- Work through agenda
- Take notes

It is important to note that not everyone will naturally embrace focus days. I once asked every employee at the company to do this exercise for one hour, pausing all work-related activities, not checking email, and silencing phones. Some employees enjoyed it, coming away with thoughts and ideas they would not have focused on otherwise. Others did not enjoy as much, as they were not sure what to think about. Some people thrive in an environment with a consistent routine with few changes daily. They may not be naturally long-term strategic thinkers and may not benefit from focus days.

By the end of your focus day, you will probably have a list of topics and notes to accompany them. They might be ideas you never thought about before and your analysis will surprise you. Taking a focus day is not easy because there is always something else you could accomplish with your time. You must remember the purpose is to put your life goals into perspective. I also created goals for every five years through the end of my life. My goals included acquiring companies and writing this book. You must set long-term goals to achieve all you want in life. The saying goes, "If you do not know where you are going, you will never get there."

Focus days are intentional times to sit down, examine what you want to do, and find a way to make it happen. They are not vacation or relaxation days because they are instrumental in establishing your big picture. I like to have focus days once each quarter. It is best to schedule all four at the beginning of the year. Worst case, if later one of the dates is no longer feasible, you can reschedule. But when you do not have any of them on your calendar, months will pass, and you will never make the time. Once you realize the benefits of your focus days, you will want to make them even more of a priority.

Start by picking a day and a distraction-free location. This location is somewhere that will help extract those big ideas and creative thoughts. Use the day to ask yourself how to improve on the things that matter most to you.

CHALLENGE

Right now schedule a focus day on your calendar.

8

Ideal Workday

How do you craft your ideal workday?

What should be included?

What would make up your ideal workday? Not the perfect day of your dreams, but if you could craft an optimal day and define exactly how you would focus and spend your time, what would it look like? When I considered this for myself, I found that the key to an ideal workday is striking the right balance between urgent and strategic. Once this is distinguished, I could dedicate the appropriate time for each.

We are experiencing an increasing need to actively respond to calls and emails, especially with a large number of employees and continuous access via cell phone. This constant demand for attention can create difficulty maintaining focus and balance during the day. Employees can also feel compromised in their ability to concentrate on important activities without balance.

An ideal workday with nine hours solely dedicated to strategic topics is not practical. It is also unrealistic to expect your ideal workday to occur daily. But being dedicated to having it at least monthly can be valuable. Not only will you accomplish a lot that day, but it can also act as a reset for your daily routine and reestablish a proper balance between what is urgent versus important.

When designing your ideal workday, dividing your work hours into specific buckets of time is helpful. How much would you allocate to different types of tasks? Again, be specific and consider the day from a minute-by-minute perspective. What would be the best balance of the tasks on your to-do list with this detailed approach?

Here is my ideal workday schedule:

8:00 - 8:15 am	Emails
8:15 - 8:45 am	Plan Day
8:45 - 9:00 am	Recognize Someone
9:00 - 9:45 am	Review Key Measures & Follow Up
9:45 - 10:15 am	Delegate
10:15 - 10:30 am	Emails
10:30 - 11:00 am	Phone Calls
11:00 - 11:30 am	Business Development & Marketing
11:30 - 12:30 pm	Strategic Projects
12:30 - 1:00 pm	Lunch
1:00 - 1:15 pm	Emails
1:15 - 2:45 pm	Projects & Meetings
2:45 - 3:15 pm	Phone Calls
3:15 - 3:45 pm	Emails

The first thing you notice is that there are no long blocks of time for strategic thinking because this activity is not feasible repeatedly. Ideal workdays should be realistic and repeatable. Conversely, in Chapter 7, "Focus Days," I discuss how these days are meant for strategic thinking only, not urgent items. You benefit from focus days most when all distractions are eliminated.

You will notice in my ideal workday I have breaks throughout for email. These dedicated times free you from the stress associated with constantly responding to email communication or wondering what you might be missing if you do not. Without permitting yourself to check your email at these specific moments in your day, you will be tempted to do so when you should be focusing on other tasks.

To create your ideal workday, start by planning. Consciously decide what projects you will work on and when during the day. This gives you clear direction instead of waiting to see what comes up. Additionally, identify whom you need to connect with during the day to plan for that effectively. Some items on the schedule are typical daily activities. Others should be more regular priorities, such as recognizing someone or connecting with a key customer or vendor. Prioritizing both typical and often overlooked tasks is important to executing your ideal workday well.

For me, there are morning and afternoon blocks of time allocated for strategic projects, addressing what is important in the long-term versus what is urgent now. The order of your day is optional. However, if there are items that frequently need to be completed, plan to tackle them in the morning. What you schedule before moving into a strategic time is crucial, as it can impact your creativity and focus. According to my schedule, the day ends at 3:45 pm. However, this is earlier than when I anticipate stopping work. I intentionally include a buffer at the end of my schedule to have extra time in case something else extends longer than initially expected. This buffer time helps keep the plan intact so the agenda is not immediately ruined when something does not go as planned.

My ideal workday schedule is not a fit for everyone, as various job positions have different responsibilities than mine. Some roles are not business development oriented or may have limited delegation ability. You must decide what the key initiatives and priorities are for your ideal workday.

The ideal workday is not to be executed to the minute, as that would be stressful and simply impossible. However, a structured timeline can help you think about your responsibilities and the time to fulfill them daily. Even if the schedule enables you to accomplish 70% of your tasks, it is still valuable because that percentage is likely higher than what you would have completed without a plan. Creating an agenda minute-by-minute sounds tedious, but it allows you to put all your responsibilities under a microscope to distinguish between urgent and important. Therefore, it is valuable to set a detailed minute-by-minute schedule, even if not followed exactly. After completing your first day, you can modify the allocation to better fit your needs for the next time better.

The schedule represents an "ideal" workday, but there are few days in a year when a person can follow it exactly as planned. But, if you fully commit to it, even for a single day, the enhanced productivity you will immediately feel and the potential for new healthy habits to form will motivate you to implement it more frequently. You will be energized to accomplish more important strategic tasks as well. However, the motivation here is also part of the challenge. How will you introduce consistency in having ideal workdays? Is it once a week or once a month? Just think about how much better your performance would be if you had a perfect workday, even once a month.

CHALLENGE

It can be hard to figure out what your ideal workday should look like. It takes focused time to contemplate priorities while remaining realistic. Spend some time defining your ideal workday and follow through with it. You will be eager to schedule it more frequently once you have experienced the results.

9

NO ONE IS OVERWORKED

Being overworked is a choice.

How do you prioritize your tasks?

Many people express that they are too busy and work too much. Ultimately it is your choice what job you have and thus how many hours you work. While a specific project or event may require additional effort and time, you can make a job change if you feel overworked. This concept is not exclusive to your career because finding balance in all areas will allow you to feel like you are in control of your life rather than it controlling you. Unfortunately, it is common to put ourselves in situations and create habits that result in a disproportionate amount of our lives spent working. If this issue plagues you, Chapter 24's "Four Steps to Breaking a Habit" will help you change behaviors that can lead you to feeling less stressed and overwhelmed.

Unless you have an assigned fixed work schedule, if we are honest, work hours are sometimes determined more by habit than need. Because of this, I intentionally allocate my time around priorities instead of trying to complete all the tasks that can be done. While working more can generate more benefits, it is impossible to do it all. Thus your decision on how many hours to work is often tied to your financial goals.

Years ago, a common manager's request to an employee was to prioritize tasks in A-B-C buckets:

A = Urgent and high-impact projects

B = Needs to get done but not urgent

C = Nice-to-do projects

However, in today's world, there are too many tasks identified as A's and B's to even consider the C's. With all the possible beneficial tasks, it is easy to feel overworked. Recognize that there is always more work than could ever be accomplished. This will help you realize you must set boundaries for your work/life balance.

I tell all employees and interviewees that if you work 60 hours a week over a long period, there is something wrong. Either, you are not properly setting your priorities, or the position contains more tasks than one person should manage. Suppose an employee has responsibilities organized well, but is still working 60 hours weekly. In that case, the company should look to hire another person, because no one should be expected to work that much over a long period of time.

In some specific industries or businesses, it is common for the business to expect and for employees to choose to work significant overtime because of financial gain. That is fine if it is based on a mutual expectation and agreement. I do not define overworked by hours, but by the feeling of working more than you want.

I recognize there are business projects and moments when extra time beyond normal is necessary. These periods of being overworked are unavoidable. This can also be true at home, where different stages of life cause you to be busier than ideal. However, in the long run, you need to decide what being overworked looks like for you, so you can recognize the signals and learn how to avoid placing yourself in such environments in the future.

How you spend your money greatly impacts your ability to control feeling overworked. Ask yourself, "How do my decisions on how I spend money impact my financial needs?" Also, "What resources do I have, and how do I use them?" If you truly prioritize not being overworked, this may result in a choice to not eat out once each week so instead you can afford to hire someone to mow the yard and do the cleaning instead. Such decisions allow you to save money in one area to save time in another. While money cannot buy happiness, it can buy the freedom to have more discretionary time.

I think of my free time as discretionary hours in which I choose to do whatever I want. If you consider your day and how many discretionary hours you have, you will realize there are few. But this also means that you can create a greater impact in your discretionary time through one small change.

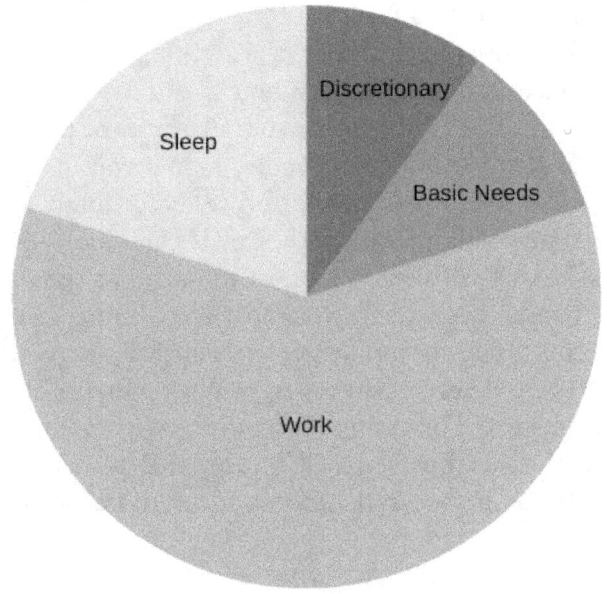

Think about your day. Subtract time spent getting up in the morning, preparing and eating meals, driving, and hours spent at work. You may end up with only 2-4 discretionary hours each day. But find a way to efficiently reduce one work hour by hiring someone to assist you, or by stopping a task. You could increase your discretionary hours by 50%. This newfound time will ease your perception of feeling overworked and positively affect the rest of your day and life.

A great tool to use to achieve more discretionary time in your day can be found in Chapter 5 on E.A.S.E., eliminate, automate, simplify, and enhance. However, it can be difficult to manage time in this fashion if your goals are monetary or for prestige. Those may require more work than you want. Even so, because you will be in charge of that choice, the perception of feeling overworked is up to you. When the choice to do more or less is just that, a choice, you retain control.

My wife is always concerned when I talk about getting involved in another business since I am already active in multiple companies. She fears the additional responsibility will reduce my discretionary hours, and I will have less family time. But I have demonstrated over time that I work a similar number of hours whether I am involved with one business or five. I rearrange priorities accordingly and my tasks change along with it. The key is consciously picking the tasks that will have the most impact. As more high-impact tasks get added, you must stop doing some less impactful tasks. As you acquire responsibilities, you must find ways to delegate, eliminate, or decide that other tasks are less critical. For example, you may have more potential A and B tasks, but you will not be able to complete as many B's as before and have to focus more on just the

A's. It is not that the B tasks have become less impactful, because they will still be beneficial. It is that you will have new more valuable tasks to accomplish that should take precedence.

Consider how you can grow and evolve in business and life. The power of choice allows you to set and reset priorities. You also have the choice to re-frame how you think about how much you work.

CHALLENGE

What is causing you to feel overworked today? The solution may just be a choice away.

10
COMPLEXITY MAY BE GOOD

Why should you embrace complexity?

Complexity can be leveraged to your benefit.

People often view complexity as stressful. It can occur when dealing with a difficult task, making a hard decision, or working with a challenging person. As a result, people tend to want to avoid complexity or eliminate it altogether. However, in business, complexity can be your friend. It can mean job security, creating customer loyalty, or providing a competitive barrier to entry. Ideally you want to reduce complexity as much as possible. But, when business is inherently complex, viewing that complexity as good can relieve a lot of stress in an organization.

For example, employees may get frustrated at being unable to quickly resolve an issue. I tell the employee that if it were easy, the company may not need their position. When looking to acquire a business, I want it to have some level of complexity, otherwise any competitor can provide the service or part. The probability of long-term success is higher if your business can master providing a complex product or service.

The benefits of complexity in a business can go beyond a product or service. If customer payment collection is complex it can be beneficial. I once talked to a client who had a large customer that generated 75 sizable invoices per year that took over 12 months to collect payment on each invoice. My client was always highly frustrated at the effort to collect every invoice. Yet after 15 years, the client has been paid over $50 million by this "difficult" customer. Yes, collections were time-consuming and complex. But because few businesses would endure the complexity of trying to collect every invoice for 12 months, this became a barrier of entry for a competitor who may have wanted to take over this customer. As a result, my client was afforded the ability to charge higher than typical pricing. In turn, the complexity generated a very profitable outcome.

Furthermore, product complexity can work to a customer's advantage as well. For example, one business I worked with only had one customer. There was no other company that could consistently meet the manufacturing specifications. This provided a win-win business model, allowing the supplier to sustain a simple business model with almost no overhead cost, so they could provide a lower cost to the customer.

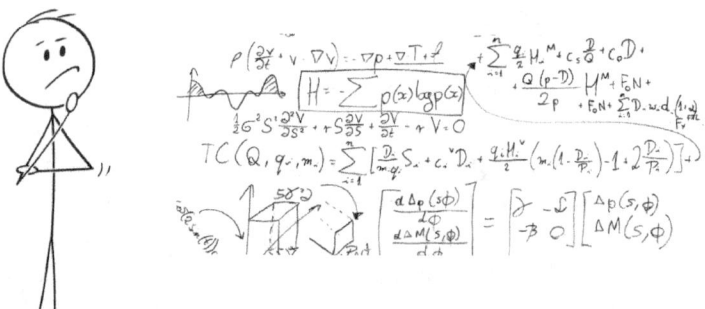

Similarly, a complex business model distinguishes you from the competition. For example, Apple Inc. designs all its products and services to work easily with other Apple products, yet they either work poorly or not at all with non-Apple devices and accessories. The company has intentionally built complexity into its brand and business model. This motivates customers to buy from Apple exclusively. As a result, they generate huge profits by charging a higher price and selling multiple products to each customer. For Apple, building complexity to buyers' alternatives has been especially valuable.

As you think about complexity in business, consider it your friend. When you have a hard day at work due to a complex issue, accepting that, in the long run, it is one of your more beneficial days will be incredibly helpful to your outlook. Keeping this mental reminder can turn a stressful event into one you are grateful for. Embracing complexity in this way can be stress relieving, motivating, and rewarding.

CHALLENGE

What is complex in your life that is causing you stress? Are there ways that in the long run the complexity may be beneficial?

11

THE MOST LOVED CUSTOMER

**Being the biggest customer does not
make you their favorite customer.**

Why is it important to be the favorite?

Suppliers are the lifeblood of many businesses, yet often, instead of encouraging relationship building, a company keeps its customers as the dominant focus instead of its vendors. I always tell my suppliers that I want to be their most valued customer. To accomplish this for yourself, think of your most loved customer and determine what characteristics have made them valuable to you, then try to be the same for your key suppliers.

As with any good relationship, it is helpful to put yourself in the other's shoes and seeing things from their perspective, especially when you encounter a product or service problem. Rather than aggressively confronting a supplier to fix something, choose to be part of the solution. Your supplier will greatly appreciate your understanding and patience. Doing so will also help build a positive relationship. Remember this when reacting: If you made the same mistake with one of your customers, how would you want that customer to respond to you?

It is important to consider costs throughout the supply chain, not just your expense. If I had an option that would add $1 to our cost but save my supplier $2, I would do so in a heartbeat because it would cause my supplier to become more profitable and increase their price competitiveness. It is important to consider all sides in price negotiations. If you approach the negotiation table with a win/lose perspective, that is all you will get. You may be the winner and your supplier the loser, but this position is sure to flip at some point in the future because suppliers need to cover their cost to make a profit. While my goal is to be a supplier's most preferred customer, I also let them know I want their best price. Often, companies demand the best price from their suppliers while making no effort to be their best customer. Buying the most volume or services does not mean you will be the most preferred. Walmart, for example, is many businesses' biggest, but typically not favorite customer. Your request for the best price will be well received and regularly acknowledged when you intentionally work to become their best customer which naturally gives you the upper hand against the competition.

Suppliers will also be more willing to accommodate you when an issue occurs if you are a preferred customer. They will bend over backward to help you, especially in an emergency. It is during a crisis when you need the support of your suppliers the most. Competitive threats, employee issues, or even a fire may become a reality in your business. I had a client whose entire lumber distribution property burned to the ground. Yet, within days, the company was back up and operating because for many years, they had been a great customer of their suppliers. Even though it cost more to help this customer bounce back from the fire, every supplier pitched in to help.

In our businesses, some of our suppliers refuse to sell products to our competitors because of our long-established relationship. I have also witnessed suppliers provide competitive market intelligence to their customers as a way of not only sharing valuable information but further solidifying long-term relationships. Great companies consider a customer-vendor relationship as a partnership because partners always seek to benefit each other.

I once had a supplier who could not operate for five weeks because a vital piece of equipment went out of commission. I contacted the supplier, and they had no other way to produce the product. Because I had an alternative supplier, I could have easily switched all my orders over to another supplier. Yet, when great companies have a hurting supplier, they find ways to help. And so, my team and I arranged for the supplier to bypass that piece of equipment, even though it meant the product would not be up to its normal specifications. Some of our customers could still easily use the product that was below normal specifications, so we separated our inventory of this product to ship only to those specific customers, allowing our supplier to still operate throughout those five weeks, with us as their only customer. Even though we had extra effort and hassle, we did not ask for a price decrease. In the end, our supplier was grateful for us as a customer who was willing to help during difficult times. This made us their most loved customer... so much so that it has been years since this occurred and our supplier's employees are still telling the story.

It may not be easy to become your suppliers' best customer, but it will always be worth it. Companies that apply this principle into their business practices will stay ahead of the competition. Short-term issues are inevitable. When working in partnership with all companies throughout the supply chain, look out for everybody's best interests, even if it causes you headaches, because in the long run, you will be more successful. Make it a goal to become your suppliers' most preferred customer. Then spend time discovering what that means and how you can accomplish it.

Challenge

Who is your favorite customer or business to work with and why?

Think of a vendor or supplier to contact to discuss ways to make collaboration easier.

12

SELLING IS STORYTELLING

Educate prospects instead of convincing them.

Past successes make great stories.

**Storytelling helps determine if the
seller and buyer are a good fit.**

Sales reps often attempt to convince the prospect, but what if selling was more about educating the prospect about the value of a product or service? I often use stories when selling because it is a great way to educate a prospect on your products, service, culture, and differentiation that provide value without resorting to a boring list of features and benefits.

Storytelling engages the prospect differently and encourages them also to share stories that will give you insight into their particular needs. While a high-push sales approach may work in certain situations and prompt short-term transactions, the prospect will not remain a customer for long unless you are bringing long-term value. Without demonstrating value, there is little potential for converting a prospect into a customer and even less for retaining that customer.

The best approach to converting prospects is one that demonstrates how you have helped others and, in turn, how you can help the current prospect reach a goal, solve a problem, or satisfy a need. If you just list features of what you are selling, this promotes an ineffective mindset where you are still trying to convince them to buy. When you instead share past customer experiences, you let the prospect know that doing business with you will exceed how your competitors perform. These stories naturally lead your prospect to tell their own stories about their needs and any potential pain they are struggling with. Sharing in this way, allows you both to decide if you are the best fit, evaluating how their needs as a potential customer could be met with what you offer.

This educational process is important in determining your business relationship. The reality is not all prospects should become customers. You may or may not be the right vendor for them. Sandler Sales Training is a popular program that centers its sales strategies in this manner. It encourages sales teams to understand a prospect's pain and determine how their company can remedy it. Suppose a prospect is not finding value from your educational discourse. In that case, you seller can move on to the next prospect, because you simply cannot persuade someone who does not need the value your company provides.

I spoke with a salesperson who, for eight years, believed that selling to a prospect meant convincing them to buy. I will never forget his look of relief when I explained that selling can be an educational process, not a convincing one. While he was always exceptional in customer support, he experienced a dramatic positive change in his approach to prospecting for new customers with this new outlook on educational selling.

Imagine you are on the receiving end of the all-too-familiar timeshare push from a high-pressure salesperson. Or maybe you have answered a door-to-door salesman's knock who begins to recite a memorized script to convince you to purchase an overpriced vacuum cleaner. We are all aware of how frustrating these experiences can be. I often wonder how they can make 50 calls daily using the "convince someone to purchase something they may not need" formula. So why do salespeople still create these stressful situations? It is not the most effective approach for either party. Ultimately no sales rep can sustain high-pressure "convincing" sales. That is why there is close to 100% turnover in such positions.

The dynamic shifts when you take an educational approach to selling and sharing your services through storytelling. Set a better tone with your prospects by letting them know immediately that you want to learn about their goals, then educate them about your product and service to see if they need it. If you are not a perfect fit, that is okay. You both took the time upfront to see if the relationship could provide mutual benefits. Because of that, there will be less pressure on the buy/sell decision. Instead, the conversation can organically build a relationship without the unattractive high-pressure sales push. This is not to say that you should tell prospects you only want to educate them. That would be disingenuous because you ultimately do want to convert them into customers… but only if they are a good fit.

So how can you increase the likelihood that a prospect will be a good fit before you initiate this conversation? After all, you do not want to spend all of your time educating without the benefit of increased sales. First, consider whether your business could be a good fit for their market. Can you provide them with additional value that your competition cannot? Once you have answered this question, you can approach prospects with your findings for their market. Share how you are different from the competition. Whether you are selling a product or service, prospects are either already buying elsewhere or you are offering something new. Confirm they need improvement in something before you attempt to sell them on your services.

One of our portfolio companies went 20 years without losing a single customer. This loyalty is because once we identified who needed our product and service, we educated them on how our company provided the best solution. When the identified need matched up with good education, it was an all-around win for our customers and for us. Because of that, every customer stayed. When approaching prospects, by getting the answers to a few questions, we could quickly determine if it was worth continuing to talk or if we should stop trying to sell them because we could not provide added value.

Leaders who tell their sales department they are not selling but rather educating through storytelling build morale and success. It lets the salesperson know it is okay not to close a sale that is not a good fit. Your sales team will quickly focus on finding those prospects who are a better match for your product or service. The initial due diligence dramatically increases the likelihood of maintaining a customer for many years. If you keep performing and the customer has a need, why would they go elsewhere?

When I use stories while selling, they are typically about prior clients or customers that show how we have added value for them. It helps to highlight how your customers had a need you could fulfill better than the competition. Stories describing how you managed a difficult situation introduce your prospects to the team and demonstrate your capabilities and integrity. You can give them a well-rounded perspective of your company through fun stories that tell more about who you are and the culture of the company. Selling as storytelling requires no pressure and no convincing. When done right, it can have a tremendous positive impact on all parties involved.

CHALLENGE

What is your favorite story about someone you have worked with? Who should hear that story?

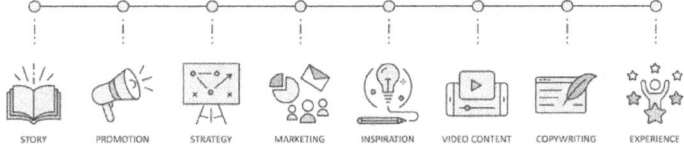

13

NEGOTIATIONS:
EVERY WORD MATTERS

When do negotiations start?

When should price be brought into the negotiations?

Negotiations begin the moment you first open your mouth. People need to recognize that every word at every stage of the process matters. What is said, how it is delivered, and the ever-present potential for a misstep are powerful negotiation determiners. Because of this, negotiations do not occur exclusively toward the end of the sales process, as it is commonly believed. They are made through the dialogue that precedes closing. The key to successful negotiations is keen and conscious awareness of the messages expressed by all parties during all discussions.

When you enter into negotiations, the initial conversations are critical. I have seen how people mistakenly believe these beginning discussions are simply meant to become acquainted or better understand the other's position. As a result, they fail to recognize the potential impact of these initial conversations. This chapter will use as an example, selling a business as a case study of all the ways every word impacts negotiations.

> "Let us never negotiate out of fear.
> But let us never fear to negotiate."
> - John F. Kennedy

Our M&A firm, Summit Advisory, has experienced seller's lack of understanding of the impact every conversation can have on the final selling price. Sellers may approach a vendor or a customer to see if they want to buy their business. Because they feel the first few discussions are only exploratory, they do not appreciate how much their words truly impact the final price. As a result, the seller makes comments they believe are harmless, never realizing they carry more weight in the long run than they expect.

A statement by the seller as simple as "my spouse is retiring in the spring" signals to a buyer that the seller will be motivated to sell before the summer to have more time to spend with their spouse. A seller may be proud to tell the buyer a story about a large project he sold, but this will result in the buyer having questions or concerns about how much of the business is reliant on the owner, even if the owner was only attempting to show why the company is growing. Simple remarks may appear inconsequential and intended to make a point unrelated to the sales negotiation. Without awareness of conclusions that could be drawn from these comments, it can be detrimental to the final selling price.

Buyers consider two components to determine the price they are willing to pay: future cash flow and risk. While cash flow is critical, the value received can fluctuate significantly based on perceived risk. Comments made by a seller often impact a buyer's perceived risk.

Another mistake sellers make in negotiations is to discuss a price range immediately. Instead, the first part of the negotiation process should always be to determine how each party can benefit from the transaction. Suppose the initial conversations are not focused on the potential synergistic or mutual gains. In that case, there is no way to know what can be achieved with a sales transaction. Only once both parties understand the post-closing benefits can either party know what is a fair price.

Summit Advisory once had a client who wanted to sell his business. He tried to sell it himself before coming to us. He met with a potential buyer on his own and shared all of his financials. He left the meeting disappointed. They only offered him $10 million when he believed the business was worth $20 million. I asked him, "What is the business worth to them?" He did not have an answer, except assuming it was the amount they offered. I asked if the potential buyer had considered all the benefits both companies would accrue if merged. He shared some theoretical ideas, but the reality was that neither party had assessed the value of the merger. As a result, a logical dollar figure for the company's value was never reached. Ultimately neither party knew what the business should be sold for because the negotiation had centered on price rather than an opportunity. Because we focused on opportunity we sold the business for over 50% more than our client initially wanted.

I was part of another transaction with an owner who had been trying to sell his business for two years. He created a detailed 40-page prospectus about his business and entertained multiple qualified prospective buyers. Yet no one offered the price he wanted. We offered to buy the company at his asking price, which was about double the actual value of the company. However, we asked for seller financing over many years. He accepted, and we were able to bring about a successful transaction because the time value of money offset the excess valuation on price. We found a way to achieve the dollar amount he wanted for his business because, through negotiations, we discovered he did not want the money upfront but preferred being paid over a long time period. The other prospective buyers unwilling to pay his asking price missed that point in negotiations and thus missed a great opportunity. This is an example of how every word matters. The transaction with us was successful because we paid attention to every word and worked to create a win-win solution. The other prospective buyers had been so focused on price that they missed seeing this opportunity.

Summit Advisory stays focused throughout an M&A process on the goals of all parties. We pay attention to every word spoken which is why we have been so successful in meeting our clients' goals and understanding buyers' goals. For over 30 years in business we have never had a transaction unwind.

This logic is why investment bankers achieve a higher selling price than if an owner tries to sell his own business. We have spoken to numerous private equity groups that buy many companies. They prefer to deal exclusively through direct contact with the business owner. They have admitted they know they will get a lower purchase price than if an investment banker represents the seller, because investment bankers know how to negotiate better.

Most people want negotiations to end with a win-win result. But those who relish trying to achieve an "I win, you lose" situation will not have long-term success. Even worse, the not-so-attractive reputation that accompanies this mentality tends to precede them as they move forward to the next endeavor. So instead, remain aware of the potentially positive and negative impact your words can have on negotiations. This will help position you to achieve what you want while understanding the best winning solution for all involved.

The discussion above concerns selling a business, but the concept is practical for other negotiations. Whether in the office with vendors or customers or at home with friends, a spouse, or children, we always negotiate with those around us. Teenagers know this and regularly use negotiating skills to their advantage. They have learned cooperation with their parents leads to a better chance of getting what they desire when negotiating for privileges. So, when your teenager suddenly starts acting like a model-perfect child, their motivation may be that they would like something from you. They intuitively understand that the first words out of their mouths leading up to negotiation with you will impact whether they get what they want.

Knowing every word counts in negotiations can help you take all conversations into account when you determine the best path for a project. It is valuable to ask as many questions as possible to learn about the other party's wants and needs. The answers can help you formulate a win-win outcome. The more significant the potential impact of negotiations, the greater you should be aware of the effect of every word.

Regardless of what is being negotiated, there must always be a conscious realization that every word creates a ripple effect. You may not see the effect in the moment. Still, it will appear later, at a more pivotal time in the negotiation process. When you understand how important this is, you can more effectively find win-win solutions by listening better to what each party desires to accomplish. You can avoid making painful mistakes and increase your chances of reaching your goals.

Challenge

The next time you are in negotiations, consider when negotiations really started and what critical considerations you must make to be successful.

*"We have an agreement in principle.
The question is, do we all have the same principles?"*

14
ACTIONS ARE POLICIES

Do your written policies represent actual practices?

Should unwritten policies be formalized?

Too often, companies think that having a written policy or procedure is sufficient. They mistakenly believe employees will follow these guidelines like a rule or law. Often the employees who are expected to follow them are not doing so. They may need to be made aware that a written policy or procedure exists in the first place. Legally and practically, if there is no consequence to ignoring a documented process, then there really is no process. If a policy dictates it is supposed to be one way, but everybody is doing something else, it does not matter what the policy says.

Even in courts of law, it does not always matter what the law states, but rather what precedents have been set in prior cases. The precedent can become the most compelling argument.

This should also be true for disciplinary action in business. When a manager decides what disciplinary action will be taken in response to employee behavior, the first question should be whether the employee was following a written policy or just what everybody else was doing.

Some personality types instinctively follow rules. If a manager has this personality type, they may believe that a policy should be followed, no matter what. A policy is a policy, after all. But is it a formal written policy or merely the accepted standard behavior? Some companies have written policies that are outdated. Still, they do not bother to change them because nobody follows them anyway.

Doing something different than following documented policies and procedures may be a good thing or a bad thing. Sometimes what everyone is doing is better than the policy in place. Evaluate both and determine if you should change the policy to match what people are doing or change what people are doing to match the policy. No procedure is truly the standard procedure unless everyone does it the same way.

A classic example for me is bedtime at our house. Julie and I decided that our son would be in bed by 10:00 PM. That was the rule, and we told our son to follow it. However, many nights he was not in bed by 10:00 PM. On one night when he was not in bed on time, Julie said we needed to discipline him for being late. Yes, we had set a policy that our son should be in bed by 10:00 PM, but he had not been doing it for the previous 30 nights, and we had not been enforcing the rule. We could not really discipline him for not getting to bed on time that particular night. It was not an issue of our son's behavior at this point; it was an issue with us as parents. The formal policy we set was not enforced or required to be followed, so the informal policy became that my son could get to bed anytime he wanted. Thus, our actions set the policy, not what we said was the policy.

Managers, just like parents, are left with the choice of retaining informal policies or starting to enforce new ones. There is no right or wrong answer to what the policy should be. The critical part is recognizing the desired policy with the best outcome, making it a documented and formal policy and reacting appropriately to any deviations. You cannot continue to work from some written policy or procedure that is not being followed or from one you merely wish was in place. Actions are policies. Just make sure they agree with what is in your company's and your customers' best interests.

CHALLENGE

Review your handbook for policies that are not followed. Determine if some policies should be changed or if action is needed to ensure compliance.

15

To Have a Great Company, You Must Have Great Meetings

What are the keys to a great meeting?

Are your meetings effective?

Meetings are the lifeblood of every organization. To gain a sense of a company's culture, attend its meetings. They are the driving force behind an organization's culture, and how participants engage in them indicates how the company operates. They require interaction between individuals and the larger organization. While one person may be able to accomplish much for the company independently, more significant impact occurs when the group can do so collectively.

So, what is the definition of a great meeting?

Several parts make up a great meeting. One is energy. Are participants enthused throughout? Are they paying attention? Are they engaged? By evaluating the team cooperation (or lack thereof) during a meeting, you can better determine the quality of that time spent together.

Another part of a great meeting is the agenda. Good leaders prepare for the meeting beforehand and ensure the agenda identifies the required topics. Great meetings have neither a delayed start nor prolonged finish.

In my meeting evaluation, I always refer to two criteria: first, what was the meeting's energy, and did it match the participants' expectations? Second, evaluate whether actionable information was created. What was the value of a meeting if there were no decisions or actions created?

A great meeting may differ between varying companies, departments, and specific projects. For example, some companies have employees that highly value social interaction. A good meeting in such a company may involve dedicated time for personal conversation. For businesses that are not socially driven, great meetings may be shorter and move directly to the agenda.

There may also be differences due to a meeting's goals. One meeting might center on brainstorming and creative collaboration. Another may carry a heavier tone, like addressing a disaster that occurred within the company. Though considerably different, both meetings can be structured to accomplish the agenda. Therefore, there cannot be one all-encompassing definition for the best meeting structure because it must fit both the situation and the participants.

Great meetings do not all operate alike, but they do all generate a result, even if it is simply getting to know co-workers better. Remember, meetings are the lifeblood of an organization. They define its culture and, as a result, are influential in determining how departments will work together and what a business's path forward will entail. A dysfunctional company often will have ineffective meetings. Leaders cannot depend on a single influential person to accomplish what can only be best done by the whole.

Too often, meetings are ineffective because they have not been adequately planned. All meetings must have preparation and an agenda. Avoiding discussing what is not on the agenda can be as important as covering what is. When I held a strategy session for a company, one of the meeting rules was that we could only talk about topics that would impact six or more months out. If someone brought up a great idea that would have an immediate impact, I would table the idea and save it for another meeting because it was outside the scope of the current meeting. This forced us to only focus on long-term initiatives and goals, which is different for most meetings. This business grew 20 percent per year for many years. It was rewarding to look back at prior strategy sessions and see how our focus during those meetings created the framework to grow the business year after year.

A healthy agenda sets the scope of a meeting and helps keep the direction on track. It can assist in curbing a meeting's length so extra time is not spent ineffectively. To ensure the agenda is followed, and everyone's input is considered, a leader's role in a meeting must be facilitator-like. In some cases, they should have no input during the meeting to avoid participants following what the leader interjects versus offering their own opinions.

A meeting's success depends on determining what information is needed and who should attend to ensure decisions can be made. Often people have good discussions, but they miss a critical topic or leave with no agreed-upon decisions, action items, or timelines. Due to a lack of note-taking, I have attended several meetings where someone brought up a topic that was already discussed in a prior meeting. Unless something had changed, the topic did not need to be revisited. Because meetings frequently go with little or no note-taking, it can be difficult to remember previous decisions and the reasoning behind them. Therefore, it is important to always have meeting documentation, set action items with assigned owners, and establish due dates.

Great meetings are important, but is it possible to have too many? To answer this question, I compare the value a meeting brings versus the sum of the value each person would have created if not attending the meeting. Suppose attendees would have more impact on the business by not being in a meeting. In that 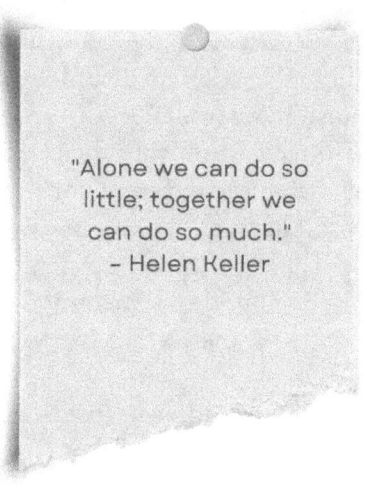 case, not having a meeting is more valuable than having one. Both having and not having a meeting may generate value, but which would generate the most value? This value assessment can also be used to decide who should attend. If one attendee can bring more value by not attending the meeting, they should not be invited. Leaders who have great meetings, capture the most value from their organization because they create more effective time spent amongst their co-workers.

"Alone we can do so little; together we can do so much."
– Helen Keller

Appreciating your employees' limited work hours will positively feed into the energy and engagement of meetings and organization culture. Without great meetings, you cannot have a great company.

CHALLENGE

Consider the last meeting you attended. Was there an agenda? Were participants prepared? Were the right people at the meeting? Were decisions and actions made? What could have been changed to make it a great meeting?

What can you or your organization do differently in the future to improve the value of meetings?

16

RESPECT IS REQUIRED
FOR LONG-TERM SUCCESS

Why is respect paramount for long-term success?

What is the link between respect and values?

Leadership styles come in all different shapes and sizes. But leaders need to obtain respect of the team to be effective over the long-term. To achieve lasting leadership success, you must prioritize earning the team's respect. Maintaining long-term and healthy respect between you and team members is critical to working well together, especially when business runs into tough times. You must depend on the relationships you have already nurtured to get past those bumps. The more respect between you and the team, the more willing they will be to go to battle with you.

You may think of historical leaders who did not have the respect of their team and yet still achieved success through a dictator leadership style. This is true, but their influence and effectiveness lasted only a short time. When leaders ignore the value of respect to compel compliance, they may achieve impressive results, but only in the short term. Over time, loyalty erodes, and success becomes difficult to sustain.

There are many ways leaders can earn respect from their team.

These include hard work, sensitivity, innovation, high intelligence, and good communication skills.

While gaining respect may not be easy, remember that it does not take much to lose what was hard-earned. Therefore, it is critical to define a personal moral compass and follow it in every action, because as a leader, people watch your every move. The commitment to gain respect may be challenging as it requires a conscious effort, repetition, and willingness to acknowledge your mistakes. But at the end of the day, the result will be worth it. Think of someone who has lost your trust. It may have resulted from a single event that caused you to feel your trust had been compromised. Thus, being consistent in your words and deeds is important. I touch on the significance of a moral compass in Chapter 30, "Truth 100% of the Time."

Plenty of articles and books exist about how leaders can cultivate great employee engagement. But those suggestions are merely words on a page if the catalyst to achieving engagement is not respect. When your employees respect you and have a fulfilling job with an enjoyable team around them, they will be engaged. Without respect, little else will matter to them. Even if everything about their job and the environment makes sense to them, respect will influence their ultimate loyalty and engagement.

This highlights the need for value alignment in business. It is a principle that ensures "everyone has the same values and understands how their goals help the organization to succeed." [12] Without it, someone may respect you as a

_____

12 Cristian Grossmann. "3 Ways to Use Value Alignment to Increase Business Success." *Beekeeper*, Sep. 6, 2022.

person but not the work situation at hand because they do not share the same beliefs or perspectives as you. What is important for one person may be unimportant for another. Trust exercises are a great way to establish a collective understanding of the team's values and your own.

Therefore, recognize what is needed to earn respect as a leader. Be aware of what the team does and does not value so you can consciously avoid disrespecting them. Respect is a two-way street. It can only be earned if it is first shown. A strong sense of respect between you and the team becomes the foundation for a kind of success that has limitless longevity.

Parenting is an additional area where respect is necessary, but one of the most challenging to achieve. The Bible reminds us "Train up a child in the way he should go; even when he is old he will not depart from it" (Proverbs 22:6, ESV). On the surface, simply telling children they must respect their parents may appear like a straightforward way to establish respect from them. However, words alone will not generate respect from your kids, as children pay more attention to your behaviors than your words. If there is an inconsistency between what you say versus what you do, whatever message you try to communicate to them will not resonate.

When children are disrespectful, intentionally or unintentionally, it can be easy to lash out and reprimand them. But pausing first to understand why they were disrespectful can be valuable. For example, you may find they were simply acting out of inexperience or lacking a perspective. Conversely, you may learn their actions were deliberate, and their disrespect was purposeful to push your buttons. Either way, you will be better educated in your discipline when you listen first, which will help you gain respect.

Whether trying to achieve long-term success at work or home, it is critical to self-evaluate whether you have earned respect. Determine what words, and more importantly, what actions are helping or hindering. Ensure there is also value alignment. The responses from those around you will demonstrate their respect for you and will greatly influence your long-term success.

CHALLENGE

Be honest with yourself and consider if there are any inconsistencies between your actions and your words. What do you need to change to have alignment?

17
THINK ON YOUR FEET

Your ability to answer quickly can build trust.

**Someone should have the ability
to provide immediate answers when needed.**

**Thinking on your feet has significant financial impact
on many negotiations.**

There are many books on how to become a great leader. However, one often overlooked dynamic is the ability to think on your feet. When faced with unexpected events, exemplary leaders have an uncanny ability to respond in ways that create positive outcomes.

We often confront situations outside our job description, without defined paths or solutions. Making logical, thoughtful, quick decisions allows you to move forward through unknown territory. How you respond in such situations can mean the difference between a positive and negative outcome and will also impact your business's ability to reach short-term and long-term goals.

Whether working with customers, vendors, or employees, quick thinking will be required. Price negotiations are often impacted by how well you think on your feet. Sending the wrong, or no message at all, can have a devastating impact. Vendors will appreciate when you can provide reliable answers instantly, especially when time is of the essence.

Being skilled at thinking on your feet can set you above the competition.

It is a different skill than used for future decision making, where you have the luxury of time and access to outside resources to inform your choice. When only seconds are available to make a decision and there is no time to process anything else, your ability to stay calm and reason will be extremely beneficial.

This skill has an even more significant impact when you are communicating with customers. When done well, your response to their inquiries builds trust in you and your company. I can recall several occasions when customers chose to continue business with our company because of how I was able to instantly respond to their questions, establishing not only business credibility, but also integrity, empathy, and mutual understanding.

When you can make a quick decision with customers, they will appreciate a quick honest response. Business is about more than just the here and now. It is about making decisions today that have a positive long-term impact, including whom to partner with, what products to buy, and what pricing to use.

The essence of this principle is ironic because the ability of leaders to effectively think on their feet now translates into future business success. Negotiations similarly depend on momentary decision-making that carries long-term influence. Successful negotiations are often the result of people who think on their feet and understand that every word matters. When neither of these concepts are present, negotiations fail, resulting from wrong information or doubt. Pair this with Chapter 13, "Negotiations: Every Word Matters," for a winning recipe at any negotiation table.

Thinking well on your feet can be a blessing, but when done poorly is a curse. Whether it is senior management officials or political leaders, we have all witnessed the consequences of someone's inability to read their surroundings and respond accordingly. Without this skill, leaders limit their influence and hinder their career potential. It can be an obstacle to progress. For an internal analyzer, thinking on their feet is a challenge. That is okay, but a calculated immediate response is sometimes needed, so consider hiring someone with this skill to be part of the team.

Thinking on your feet as a leader directly affects the team's respect for you. Constant indecisiveness will paint you into a corner and cause respect to weaken over time. When confronted with an employee's personal issue, you will need to respond immediately. A genuine response of empathy will go a long way in building trust and making you a great leader.

When selecting people for leadership positions make it a priority to evaluate the applicant's ability to think and respond quickly. Consider your own abilities to think on your feet when needed.

CHALLENGE
What aspect of a situation impacts whether you are good or poor at thinking on your feet?

18

THINKING INTO THE FUTURE

Is it better to see the forest or the trees?

**Is an underperforming employee
a bad fit for the company?**

What positions require a different thinking horizon?

People are wired differently on how far into the future they focus. Thinking about the present comes naturally to some. Others enjoy thinking far into the future. In business, some roles are best suited for present-day thinking and others are best filled with future thinkers. It is important that an employee's natural tendency in forward thinking be aligned with their job's focus requirements. People working on production lines should have a short horizon focus and must concentrate on each part before them to perform well. However, the company president should not focus only on the current day but rather on where the company needs to be far into the future.

In his book *Good to Great,* Jim Collins captured the importance of matching skills with roles using a metaphorical "bus." The people who make up the business they work for are on this bus. He emphasized how significant it is for the right people to be in the right seats (job/position) that match their skill set. However, he missed the aspect of employee focus. Some people focus on the here and now, which is great for some positions but ineffective for others. Many managers and human resource departments concentrate so much on a skill they overlook the importance of matching an employee's time horizon thinking with the optimal horizon focus of each position.

Thus, you need to hire people with the right skill set and whose outlook matches the needs of the position they are filling. For example, while it makes sense for a production line worker to focus only on today, the same should not be true for a foreman. The foreman will need to consider next week's schedule and future staffing and materials needs. While the production employees and foreman are taking care of the next few weeks, the plant manager must focus 2-3 months ahead to ensure production and sales have the necessary resources. Meanwhile, the president needs to focus on anticipating market changes, required capital, and assuring adequate financing. If the president gets caught up in the day-to-day, no one will be planning for the business's long-term success. As the famous saying goes, presidents and owners should focus *on* the business, not *in* the business. Chapter 22, "Greatest Strength Is Also Greatest Weakness," describes how someone's strengths can be an asset in one environment but a liability elsewhere, which can be true when comparing employee outlook versus the outlook needed for a particular role. I have seen employees perform very well and get promoted but then be less successful in their new role, which requires an outlook the person is not comfortable with.

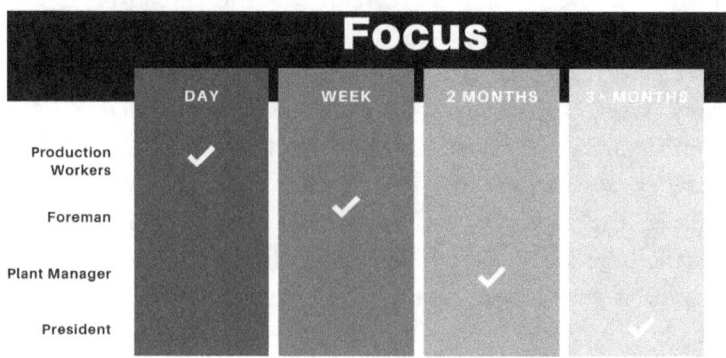

Sometimes it is best to pair up opposites. With their sight set on the bigger picture, employees in roles requiring them to focus on the future may overlook what is immediately around them. Think of this as a forest. Some do not see the individual trees, while a second set of eyes that are near-term focused can intuitively factor in those details. The two can work together to fill in what the other might miss, achieving better results.

Underperforming employees are not always a wrong fit for the business. They may be positioned poorly and not able to exercise their full potential. They might have a valuable timeline outlook, but only for a different position. It is all a matter of where their perspective will thrive best. Great leaders need to recognize mismatches and make adjustments, but also intentionally work to avoid placing an employee in an uncomplimentary role from the beginning.

Some companies struggle during growth because the owner/founder, who may have been excellent with details, never planned for something greater. As a result, the business is often successful up to a certain size, but once it begins to grow larger and more complex, it noticeably struggles to function effectively. My experiences show there are very defined levels that require a different style of management. I have been a part of many business transitions as part of our investment banking firm. It amazes me how many businesses are successful up to $1M but then need a new owner to grow. The need for another ownership change happens again at $8M, which requires a more structured organization to expand beyond this level.

In a mom-and-pop business, every detail has your fingerprints on it. Once your business grows to $1M, the need for staff and structure increases. Owners can function in an environment they are familiar with, but to get to the next level, they need to remake themselves or hire others with complementary skills and outlooks. The customer mix becomes more complex, employee development and departmental management needs become a higher priority, and these pivotal shifts are necessary for expansion. Once $8M is exceeded, the company may struggle again to fit into a new business model and management style that is needed to grow beyond the current threshold. This requires a transformation, new hires, or selling the business to an owner with a new style and skill set.

Whether managing people or looking at your own life, consider how far into the future a particular task or role requires you to look. Does it match your personality and skill set, or is it meant for someone else? College graduates should be especially aware of this topic as they evaluate how far into the future they focus and what positions match their outlook. This will help them move into a career path with a higher chance of long-term success. In addition, prioritizing this concept in your life, hiring practices, and career decisions will assure greater success and fulfillment.

CHALLENGE

Analyze one of your roles or tasks. Does your natural time horizon thinking match what is needed?

19

Drill Sergeant or Grandpa

Are you motivating the team appropriately?

**A leader's style must match how
team members want to be led.**

Leaders tend to adopt one of two styles of leadership. One is more like a drill sergeant, while the other can be more like a friendly grandpa. The drill sergeant takes on a dictator leadership style, while the Grandpa style takes on more of an encouraging tone. However different they may be, they can both be successful. The key is ensuring the leadership style matches what motivates the team members. Some people perform better with supportive feedback, while others need a high-energy, kick-your-butt type of leader to drive them forward. It is all a matter of coupling the leadership style to those who will receive it.

I find it interesting when a professional coach, who is ineffective with one team, becomes highly successful with another. In most cases, this change in results is not because the coach changed his approach or his abilities improved. He has instead found team members who respond better to his coaching style. A new coach often has an initially high degree of turnover among players as he puts together a team that fits his mold. Great players were released because they did not adapt to the new coach's style. In the end, the team is highly successful when a group of players responds well to the coach's style and collectively concede to a singular culture. Steve Kerr of the Golden State Warriors and Bobby Knight of the Indiana Hoosiers are examples of basketball coaches with noticeably different coaching styles but, both have been highly successful. Bobby Knight was often overbearing and known to scream at his players. Steve Kerr is calmer and more encouraging. If you kept the team members the same but flipped coaches, neither team would have been successful.

I have two daughters who both played soccer. One performed well with a coach who encouraged and offered plenty of praise. The other responded best to an assertive coach who motivated the players by yelling at them. Some might argue that coaches should change to match their players. But that is like someone telling you to change your personality. It simply does not work that way. Leadership styles must be considered when assembling a team and choosing a leader. As discussed in Chapter 22, "Greatest Strength is Also Great Weakness," you may be a great fit on one team but a weak fit on another.

Teams and coaches develop a culture over time. This does not come about through a once-and-done decision. The result can be a mismatch between the leadership style and what is preferred according to the team members' motivational needs. When this happens, it is important to recognize the dynamic clash. To have the best chance at long-term success, leaders must take the time to evaluate the best culture for the team. This style may remain consistent for considerable periods of time. However, an unexpected event might require a different style to lead a company through a crisis. This may require a temporary change in who is leading the team, to a leader that is more short-term focued. Once the crisis has been resolved, be sure leadership is returned to the prior style to continue guiding the company as before.

Whether your leadership style is more of a drill sergeant or a grandpa approach, remember that one is not more effective than the other. Both can be successful, but only in the right environment that matches how the team members respond best.

CHALLENGE

Think about a team you are on and decide if the leadership style matches how team members are best motivated.

20
EMPLOYEE HIERARCHY

What is equal treatment in a business?

All words matter.

"All employees are treated equally here." It is the sentiment commonly promoted amongst companies and their leaders. However, I contend that even the best of them have yet to master this concept fully. While policies and actions may support this in theory, the nuances of communication within organizations do not consistently demonstrate the principle. Employee morale is jeopardized when subtle differences in treatment are tolerated. Listening closely to employee dialogue and looking deeper into the business culture may reveal the reality that not everyone is treated equally.

One of the first places to look is the employee parking lot. It can send a counterintuitive message when reserved spaces exist for certain employees. This clearly indicates there are people in the organization who are more important than others and deserve preferred parking as a result of their significance. An organization chart, where people are arranged positionally from top to bottom also challenges how employees are truly regarded. The chart is often not only a reflection of a company's culture but also why some managers talk down on the organization. Their words and tone can emphasize employee hierarchy.

A simple list of employees replaces traditional organization charts in our companies. I want everyone to feel they are equally valued, with no single person or people above others. Each person has a role to play, different parts that make up strong teams and in, turn, a robust business. If everyone is treated as equally valued, they will believe it is true. They will be more willing to participate freely and share their input without fear of not being heard or respected. People will want to go beyond the call of duty because they instinctively know that what they offer matters and is valuable.

People need to feel empowered and expected to contribute. I inform all new employees that something is wrong if they have not disagreed and challenged me in the first six months of their employment. Either they are scared to challenge my opinion or they are blindly following what I have said. Both cases are an issue, so they must feel encouraged to express their viewpoint. When there is a difference in opinion, we will discuss it until resolved. About 90 percent of the time, we come to a mutual agreement on next steps. For the remaining 10 percent, when we cannot agree, 9 out of 10 times, I will go with their opinion and concede to their perspective. The few times when my opinion will trump others is if there is a significant risk/reward with the outcome and I need to ultimately decide to take the risk or not.

Another way people push a culture of hierarchy is by how they refer to their co-workers. I cringe when I hear managers use the language "my team" or "my employees." While they may not intentionally mean anything by it, the statement comes across with an ownership perspective rather than acknowledging the unit as a team with equal value. Terms like "the team," "our team," "employees on the team," or "employees in our department" are better descriptors to emphasize that no one is more important. For this reason, I do not allow employees to call or introduce me as their boss, as this often causes them to believe my opinion carries more weight than theirs.

While everyone should be valued equally, everyone does not impact the business equally. Some employees can have a much bigger impact than others. However, no one can be successful on their own and make a notable difference without the support of others. Team members must understand everyone's roles individually to best appreciate their impact as a whole, with zero consideration for hierarchy. There can undoubtedly be leaders within a team who help organize and direct strategy. That is a role they play which can significantly impact the team's success, but everyone on the team has their role that supports the company's success. I do not care how great of a coach a football team has. The coach will not be successful if every player is not valued for their contribution to the team.

Unfortunately, in large corporations, there are generally large egos. In some cases, the ego helped them get there. But to do something great in the long run, their ego will eventually get in the way. These individuals would hinder any attempt to eliminate the hierarchy. They are attached to how many employees they manage instead of viewing themselves as just another team member. Because of this, they clearly place misguided value on their title, which only feeds the perception commonly associated with a hierarchy of job titles. To avoid this, we do not care about job titles in our companies. Most of our employees make up their own job titles to use when communicating with customers and vendors. We do not pay based on a hierarchy of titles. This principle began early in my career. I once attended a networking event where I was introduced without my title and shook hands with an individual who then ignored me. When she found out my title later, she reintroduced herself to me and shook my hand again. She treats people with certain titles in a special way and does not view everyone equally. Thus, the only time we use titles is if the other person needs to understand which department of a company someone works in.

Policies are important as they set the tone for your business culture. For more insight on setting policies, check out Chapter 14, "Actions Are Policies." The language used around your employees affects them more than what is written on the company's mission statement. Maybe you need to self-reflect and challenge your regular use of the term "my employees." Perhaps individuals are coming to mind as you read this who have not felt comfortable sharing their thoughts in meetings. You will have greater success if everyone around you believes that everyone should be equally valued.

CHALLENGE

Evaluate your company. Assess its structure, policies, and the language being used among employees. Are all employees equally valued?

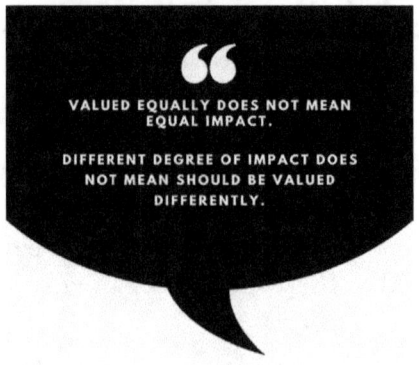

VALUED EQUALLY DOES NOT MEAN EQUAL IMPACT.

DIFFERENT DEGREE OF IMPACT DOES NOT MEAN SHOULD BE VALUED DIFFERENTLY.

21

THE VALUE OF CHECKING REFERENCES WHEN HIRING NEW EMPLOYEES

It is more than just "were they a good employee?"

What questions should you ask?

How can you use references to improve onboarding?

Contrary to popular belief, references should not be used to solely verify if an applicant was a good employee elsewhere. It might be valuable to a degree, but everyone knows the references provided will likely have good things to say about your applicant. Employers should instead approach references with two goals:

1. To confirm or deny your suspicions and concerns about the applicant.

2. To find out what will make this individual successful post-hire.

By asking the right questions and engaging references well, you can receive more than just typical responses. It may be helpful to understand what environment the applicant works best in. Understanding your applicant's preferences from their references is valuable whether hiring for a company, board of directors, or a committee position. Ideally, you want to talk with someone who has worked with the applicant in a similar environment to the job you are trying to fill. For this reason, I find references that are just friends to be less valuable. Once, I had an applicant list his wife as a reference, which I found comical. That could be dangerous for the applicant, as the wife may not be a good reference if he did not clean the dishes the night before. This was a reference we did not call.

One of my goals when speaking with references is to understand what work environment would make the applicant most successful. This can be anything from working independently, on a team, or somewhere between. Additionally, references can reveal your applicant's ability to be self-motivated, how well they perform under pressure, and how much experience they have with a specific task or responsibility. When talking with references, consider asking them these questions about your applicant:

- Do they need to be given much direction, or prefer to work on projects with little guidance?

- What type of managers are they, or have they never managed before?

- What type of tasks do they flourish at?

- How do they add or subtract energy from a team?

The purpose here is to find out if your environment is a good fit, and if it is, whether you can also provide the support needed for them to reach a higher level.

Through this questioning of references, you can validate perceptions of the applicant you developed during the interview process. As the reference shares examples and stories about this person, you can use those to either confirm or dismiss your perceptions.

I have called references to address a specific concern noted in the interview process. The conversation affirmed that the applicant would only be successful in a different situation than what we could offer. I quickly determined that while the applicant may be a great employee in a different setting, they would not be a good fit for our company.

An applicant may need to be stronger in the traits you seek. With the right questions, you can determine this before you hire. People ask references, "What are the applicant's greatest strengths and weaknesses?" Since I have yet to find a reference willing to talk about someone's weaknesses, I adjust the question the following way. "All of us have things we need to improve upon. What would be the one thing this applicant could improve to make a greater impact?" This is a question they are willing to answer, which provides valuable feedback.

Contacting references can also be a way to verify what is listed on resumes since these documents are often exaggerated. You can ask about the reporting structure, tasks completed, or an applicant's role on a particular project. In some cases, it can be enlightening to ask what percent of an accomplishment listed on the resume was due to the applicant's efforts. Sometimes I find the applicant was only a minor contributor to a team and had a minor impact on the noted accomplishment. If you receive a resume with a lack of good references or are having trouble reaching one or more of them through the contact numbers provided, that should be an immediate red flag.

The ideal reference should be someone with whom the applicant is currently employed. The second best is someone connected to a previous workplace. Ideally, you want to speak with a direct supervisor, not a co-worker.

Keep in mind you should not contact an applicant's current company without the applicant's consent.

Any reference will be more willing to provide detailed feedback if you give them background on the position you are filling and why you are interested in this applicant. If talking with the applicant's current employer, I take this opportunity to express our willingness to provide flexibility in a transition period. They appreciate my concern about ensuring a smooth transition out of their current role. From my perspective, since my approach is as if I am "hiring for life," it is not a big deal to wait a few extra weeks to allow the candidate time to ensure a smooth exit from their current company. The reference will appreciate you demonstrating that this is not all about you. Sometimes, when talking with references, I have even found they are potential customers. Hence, when you ask the right questions, references can become the gateway to more than simply addressing whether a candidate will become a good employee.

To respect a reference's time, who has little to gain by talking with you, try to keep the conversation as short as possible. Since you only have a few minutes, you need to have a specific plan for what you want to accomplish on the call. For example, you may want to better understand why candidates are leaving their current job, or why they are no longer a fit with that company. Maybe you want to find out why they were not considered for a different role within their current company. Through these conversations, you can learn more about their skill sets, what they may be lacking for their current position, and what they can potentially bring to the role you are hoping to fill.

Because it can be time-consuming to call numerous references, you might be tempted to skip it entirely when you are exhausted from the search process. Do not give in to the temptation because those references can be extremely valuable in helping you avoid costly mistakes. We have had applicants we initially believed would make great hires. However, our positive perspective quickly changed for reasons only made aware to us through their references.

Remember, you are also trying to set up applicants for post-hire success. A reference's first-hand experience is your only chance to learn something about the applicant you may not have discovered otherwise. Therefore, you must force yourself to take the time to call multiple references. It will always be a discipline worthy of your commitment. It is rewarding to make a hire and feel confident you can paint a comprehensive picture of the applicant's strengths, development needs, best-fit working environments, and so much more, because you have intentionally engaged with their references to determine what mutual success would look like.

CHALLENGE

What questions will you ask references for your next hire?

What do you wish you would have known about your last hire?

BEYOND THE DESK

22

GREATEST STRENGTH IS
ALSO GREATEST WEAKNESS

Do you know when your strength is working against you?

**Do you know what situations you should avoid
because they are not suited for your skill set?**

We each possess characteristics and skills that we view as
strengths or weaknesses. In some areas, we feel extremely
confident. Conventional wisdom teaches that we should
focus on operating only from these strengths and delegate
tasks to others for areas in which we are weak. While
this is a solid strategy, it is important to recognize that
your greatest strength in one situation can equate to your
greatest weakness in another.

For example, a person with a dominant personality may be
well suited to be a leader, setting direction and strategy for
a team. That can be a massive benefit in a military conquest
if they are the leader. However, imagine the disarray if

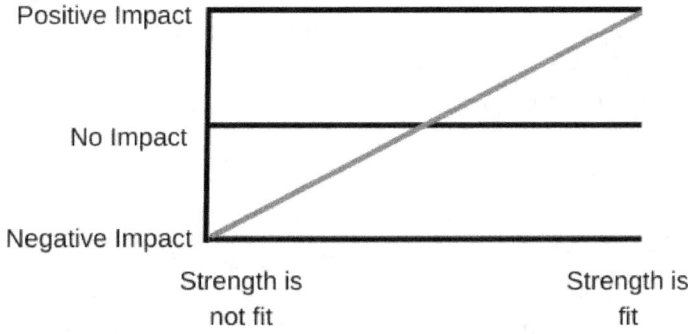

everybody in the military unit had the same leadership strength. Each would strategize independently on how to win the war, and there would be no cohesion. Thus, if a unit had ten strong dominant leaders, they would cause chaos if they could not follow instructions of the commander. Instead, all ten of them would try to use their strength as a leader, which in this situation, would be a weakness to achieving the unit's goals.

Strengths that make someone a great leader sometimes do not translate well at home with a spouse and children. Sometimes at home they need to just be a listener, building up their spouse, or allowing children to solve problems for themselves. While their leadership skills are hugely successful at work, this strength at work is a weakness at home.

Match your greatest strengths to the best situations to utilize them. It is often hard to hold yourself back when a strong characteristic you want to contribute is not beneficial in a particular situation. For example, sometimes you are not the subject matter expert and should allow someone else to take the lead. Also, understand that different personalities are all valuable. No one type of personality is better than any other in all situations.

Certain sports coaches are successful with a particular team or player. This is because they know how to use team members' strengths for the greater good of the team. Coaches have to change their call playing when the team members change so they can leverage the new player's strengths.

Years ago, the business philosophy was to develop your weaknesses. Annual employee reviews would identify your weakness and create plans to fix it. However, the

Gallup publication, *Now, Discover Your Strengths,* talks about how the focus should be on your strengths, and that is what you should work on, not your weaknesses. Only work on a weakness if it gets in the way of your strengths. Even then, only work on getting those skills up so that your weaknesses no longer hinder your strengths. In one study, Gallup found that employees feel more confident, self-aware, and productive when focusing on strengths rather than weaknesses. This leads to higher employee engagement, increased performance, and significantly lower attrition rates. [13]

Some situations call for thinkers and ponderers, while others require a decision to be made instantly. These are two different skill sets. We know opposites attract, which can sometimes cause frustration but provides a broader skillset. In relationships with coworkers, children, or a spouse, you can start to learn how to balance and offset each other's strengths and weaknesses.

Young adults may need help to identify their greatest strengths. It can be difficult to determine what job or career to go into without the ability to recognize situations in which they can be most successful. Young adults will be more successful if they choose a career that requires their strengths. It is important to know where our strengths fit in and make conscious decisions to acknowledge situations that would be best to avoid or delegate to others.

In families, it can be helpful to have a level-headed parent who can think through issues strategically without getting emotional. In a disaster, this parent remains calm and

---

13 https://www.gallup.com/workplace/242096/focus-people-strengths-increases-work-engagement.aspx

guides others to solutions. Conversely, this strength is a weakness when a child shares something they are excited about. This parent may seem detached or aloof because they do not demonstrate a significant emotional response. There is no cheering, hooting, hollering, or laughter. The child may wonder if the person was even listening. Thus, it will be beneficial if there is a second parent whose strength is more emotional responses. The more emotional parent can connect better with their child's emotions.

Consider how to match up your greatest strengths to the right situations. Next, become more aware of activities for which your strength may instead be a detriment. Finally, recognize other people's strengths and weaknesses and observe how they are beneficial or detrimental in different activities.

Personality tests, like the Myers-Briggs Type Indicator, have been used for many years to help identify personality characteristics. Using answers to a series of questions, it develops a summary description of how you act and react and the best function in the world. The Indicator has 16 options based on scales between Extroversion and Introversion, Sensing and Intuition, Thinking and Feeling, and Judging and Perceiving. It can be a valuable tool to help you determine your strengths and in what situations you will flourish. It can also be a great tool to assist you in selecting team members that will work well together on a project.

Take the time to evaluate your strengths and weaknesses. Consider when it is appropriate to use your strengths and when applying them can cause more harm than the good you intend. Always be mindful of the strengths of those around you.

CHALLENGE

What is your greatest strength and for what project is it great for?

23
THINK RIGHT, ASSUME WRONG

**Are you confident enough
to consider you could be wrong?**

**Can employees, family, and friends
challenge you without fear?**

**The next time someone questions your decision,
hear them out...even if you think you are 100% right.**

People should enter situations thinking they are right but assuming they may be wrong. This chapter is not about determining when people are correct or incorrect. It is more about adopting an attitude of acknowledgment for the possibility of learning something new that may change your mind.

Successful people can believe they are right, but for others not to view them as egotistical, they need to be open-minded about the possibility that they may be wrong. Too often, people participate in conversations believing they are right and thus are closed to new ideas. There is no greater blatant example of everyone believing they were right than when people considered the Earth was flat, until they found new information that proved them wrong. If an entire society can be so inaccurate about the shape of the planet, there is a chance one of your beliefs could also be misguided.

Leaders should have strong beliefs. But what makes them great is that they are open to learning new data that could change their conclusions. Good leadership must discern if decisions are based on all available facts or just opinions. Today, people consume a great deal of information on social media. A negative of that medium is that anyone can express what they believe as if it were fact. It becomes challenging to distinguish fact from opinion, especially when there is no one filtering the information.

Previously, when the most common forms of communication were limited to books, newspapers, and television, an editor held ultimate responsibility for the content's validity and would do the work necessary to ensure it was sound. These days, everyone is their own editor, and what they share with the world is always presumed right in their eyes. If you have ever listened to two good lawyers argue the same case, you quickly discover they can easily shift your beliefs. You can be convinced of what the right verdict should be once the plaintiff presents their position. However, after you hear the defense, its presentation can completely change your mind about the "correct" verdict. This demonstrates that additional facts or perspectives can change your mind.

Because I typically do not share input until after I have taken the time to think through my answers, I feel confident in my answers. Some people can perceive this self-confidence as having an attitude of a know-it-all. However, once people have been around me long enough, they realize I am open to learning new facts and perspectives and am willing to change my mind.

Sometimes newer employees may not voice their disagreement with me because I am the "President."

It takes time for them to discover that pushing back is welcome and expected. Once they see me change my mind because of their input, they begin to understand that no one's opinion has more value than another, regardless of job title. Rather than titles, facts and experience are what weigh more heavily in the decision-making process. People who are willing to be wrong and permit others to challenge their stance become more effective leaders.

Great leaders create a work environment expectation where people have permission to challenge. However, doing so disrespectfully is unacceptable. Common courtesy allows for healthy and open dialogue when a new idea is suggested. It helps to view all communication as a learning opportunity. Either you are going to learn something new, or you will reaffirm current beliefs. Two people can agree to disagree, but acknowledging and understanding the other's stance still offers a learning opportunity.

For debate team competitions, it is a common preparatory practice to defend both sides of an argument. This requires the debaters to research both sides of an argument to understand all potential viewpoints. Remember, intelligent people, are not solely those with high IQs. They are also those who intentionally interact with others and constantly increase their knowledge as a result.

Abraham Lincoln was once approached by a statesman with a concern: "Mr. President, one of your other statesmen has said some negative things about you." After disclosing what this fellow statesman expressed, the President did not respond. Instead, he stood up, took his coat and hat, and left his office. "Where are you going, Mr. President?" the statesman asked. "I am going to talk to that man because he usually knows what he's talking about." The point here is this: Everyone has blind spots preventing them from seeing the whole picture. Whether it is about us, others, or a situation, people should not conclude something for which they do not have all the information or fully understand.

Sometimes at work, people assume behaviors are solely due to attitudes. If we must address a person's poor conduct, we may immediately think it is attitude related. However, remember to assume you could be wrong. In the past, I have approached an employee to discuss corrective actions for poor performance. Luckily, I entered the conversation with an open mind about what might be causing the poor performance. I learned that the recent out-of-character behavior had been related to caring for a severely sick child. If I had disciplined them because I thought I had all the facts, I would have come across as an inconsiderate person. Becoming sensitive to what is happening in your employees' lives helps you maintain awareness to direct your management style positively. Assuming you are wrong is an attitude. Leaders are comfortable with making a decision they feel is right, yet nothing is worse than realizing you are wrong when it is too late to change.

What would happen if we all adopted this attitude while driving? Not everyone on the road with you is as terrible of a driver as you may think. That "idiot driver" may be rushing to a hospital or facing another emergency. In most cases, you may be correct that they are just reckless, but in some cases, you may be wrong in assuming they do not have a justifiable reason for their behavior.

I learned this lesson over 25 years ago when I was leaving the office one day. The car in front of me pulled halfway into the intersection, heading left, but stopped. I was frustrated that someone would dangerously stop in the middle of an intersection. I went around her and realized the driver was a woman who worked in my office. The next day, I learned that she had not chosen to stop in the middle of the intersection; her car had broken down at that very spot. I would have made a fool of myself if I had shown my frustration to her when I passed her the day before. I will always remember this event because you never know what the person next to you is going through.

As parents, we have beliefs about our kids and hold them as true. Yet, we must be willing to seek out the information needed to confirm those beliefs and not resist change if our search proves us wrong. As stated in the Broadway production of *Newsies*, "Being [a leader] does not mean you have all the answers, just the brains to recognize the right one when you hear it." [14] Some moments are meant to gather the necessary facts. Attitude will determine how the situation develops. If a leader believes they are right with no room for error, the outcome can be ineffective.

When dealing with customers, be cautious of your thought process. Thinking you are right, but assuming wrong is a crucial mentality for exceptional customer service. I have been in many situations where employees assumed customer's complaint of a product issue was simply due to the customer utilizing the product incorrectly. Upon further investigation, the employees found their assumption was false after somebody discovered a defective part, or inaccurate instructions had been sent to the customer.

One mental exercise to adopt when attempting to refrain from considering your assumptions are correct is to analyze

---

14 Menken, Alan. (2012). *Disney's Newsies*: The Broadway Musical, New York.

the data presented. Ask yourself, "What parts of the data could be wrong, or what about my assumptions may be false?" This devil's advocate approach can open your mind to the possibility that you may not have all the necessary facts.

As you make a decision, it is important to consider the impact of coming to a false conclusion. Some wrong decisions have minimal impact, so you can move forward with limited input. Meanwhile, others can be extremely impactful and might lead to terrible outcomes, even death. The Space Shuttle Challenger tragedy resulted from groupthink theory at play where a group of brilliant scientists believed a plan was accurate. No one dared to challenge the group consensus. They also refrained from addressing safety concerns for fear of an unfavorable reaction to their disapproval. As a result of working in an environment that restricted employees from challenging the status quo, seven astronauts lost their lives.

What price are you willing to pay to be right, even when you may be wrong? Great leaders must be willing to have others challenge them because there is so much value in allowing others to point out what you may not be able to see. If people know you are willing to be wrong, they will be more open to presenting new information. They will also engage more because your openness aids their comfort.

Leaders who adopt a philosophy and attitude of "I think I am right but may be wrong" are dramatically different from those who do not. It is easily noticeable in tonality, body language, willingness to hear all perspectives, questions asked, and how they listen. Good leaders will pick up more information in a conversation and know how to drill down for new data effectively and sensitively when necessary. I have been in group discussions where one small comment dramatically changed the course and outcome of the conversation. If that person had been unwilling to speak up, the outcome would not have been as good.

Thinking you are right but assuming you are wrong starts with an open mind. While it allows you to be confident in your opinions, it provides the opportunity to pivot in your opinions and to value the input of others.

CHALLENGE

For the next few days, in conversation, assume your perceptions are wrong and really listen to the other person.

24
Four Steps to Change a Habit

Habits are hard to change, but recognizing these four steps will improve success.

Habit:
A settled or regular tendency or practice, especially one that is hard to give up.[15]

Everyone has bad habits they would like to change. The challenge is finding a way to successfully make it happen, as reversing a habit involves both behaviors and psychology. Unfortunately, most people struggle and ultimately give up trying to change. To help you succeed, I have created this four-step system you can use to finally make tangible progress toward becoming the best version of yourself.

Step 1: Commit
The first step is committing to make a very specific change. You cannot be vague such as, "I want to be a better spouse." Instead, you must identify a particular action, thought, or verbal occurrence you want to modify or completely stop. For example: "I want to stop complaining about work." Your desire must also be genuine and accompany your commitment to follow through with whatever is necessary. Without such a mental shift, you will remain stuck at step zero. It is not enough to wish for change; you need adamant determination.

---

15 https://www.lexico.com/en/definition/habit

Bear in mind that not all habits are negative. Some are valuable parts of life, like the habits of prayer or exercise or brushing your teeth before bed. After you identify the harmful habit you would like to shift, list all the benefits that will follow as a result of your success. Looking forward to the transformation can help motivate you to continue.

STEP 2: NOTICE THE REPETITION

Now that you have chosen to be dedicated to changing a specific habit, you will naturally become more aware of when it occurs. You will begin to experience lightbulb moments, catching yourself after you have repeated the habitual behavior. Recognizing the repetition of a habit is a significant milestone toward solidifying its change. At this step, you may still complain about work, but you will immediately catch yourself after complaining. Part of the value of these four steps is recognizing progress. Many people will give up at step 2 because they have been unsuccessful at breaking the habit. Instead, consider yourself successful in that you immediately recognize the behavior you want to change. Typically you will remain in step 2 for a period of time, repeating the habit but recognizing when you do it.

STEP 3: NOTICE IT HAPPENING

As it becomes more conscious and common for you to notice the behavior after the fact, you can naturally migrate into step 3, where you recognize the habit as it occurs. Whether the tendency you want to change is something you say or something you do, you reach this step when you notice yourself while committing the behavior. Instead of catching yourself after complaining about work, you will start to catch yourself mid-sentence.

Be patient. It will take time to get to this point. The habit has gone uninterrupted for a long while, so it is easy to continue. Do not beat yourself up or get discouraged. Instead, applaud yourself each time you notice the behavior. Allow this new awareness to encourage your forward movement. Change is not instant. As basketball coach John Wooden once said, "Good things take time, as they should... Getting something too easily or too soon can cheapen the outcome." [16] Remember to give yourself grace and celebrate your progress.

STEP 4: STOP YOURSELF BEFORE IT HAPPENS

Eventually you will move to step 4, which is catching yourself before doing the behavior. You will start to think about complaining about work, but will stop before you start. As part of moving from step 3 to step 4, you can now become conscious of the kinds of situations which prompts the habit. During step 4 of this change process, you need to understand what has triggered the habitual behavior in the past so you can instead be mindful and catch yourself before the habit surfaces again. It is a great feeling when you are ready to repeat the habit, but you stop before you do, confirming you have reached this milestone achievement.

It is common to notice yourself slipping back to step 3, even after progressing in step 4. Again, do not let anything discourage you. Instead, remind yourself that you are accomplishing something difficult but rewarding. Over time you will stop slipping back to step 3 and stay in step 4.

---

16 *The Greatest Coach Ever: Timeless Wisdom and Insights of John Wooden.* Gospel Light Publications, 2010.

At this point, you will be confident that you have successfully changed a habit, which by definition, is hard. You will have accomplished something that many people do not. But it will only happen if you are cognizant of each step in the process.

Start Today!

Three to four months is the approximate amount of time needed to change a habit fully. The countdown begins once you fully commit to step 1 and have the right mindset. Now that you understand the steps necessary to reach your goal, remind yourself of all the benefits you will feel once you achieve this personal transformation. With discipline and time, you can replace undesirable behaviors with positive habits that effortlessly become a natural part of your life.

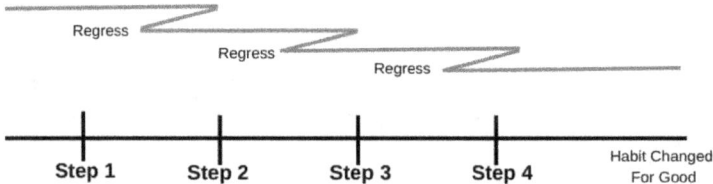

Challenge

Pick one habit you would like to eliminate and decide if you are willing to commit to changing it.

25

Conflict Due to Lack of Facts

Conflict does not have to be stressful or negative.

Start with the perceptions of each party.

People can better resolve conflict by understanding all the facts. When a solution is hard to come by, it usually means information about the reason behind each party's behaviors is still missing. Identifying and communicating all the facts can bring about tremendous clarity. While establishing the contributing factors may not immediately solve all conflicts, it is a great place to start.

Often we mistakenly assume others share the same understanding and context on a topic. This is especially true in an office where everyone shares the same space and hears the same communication. However, people learn and listen differently. For example, if you were to ask five people who witnessed an automobile accident to describe the event, studies have shown you would receive five different responses. Therefore, people do in fact have varied interpretations because of perspective, a missed connection, or a lack of information. Frustration and disagreements continue until all parties understand and

appreciate each other's points of view before they can work toward a resolution.

Conflict is bound to occur where there are different motivations, attitudes, and personality types. Therefore, ongoing situations need to be addressed as a system rather than as individual events. Yet, understanding what facts are known and unknown is event-specific. It may be related to the different personality types involved in the situation.

Suppose there are fundamental differences between two people. In that case, you need to either set up rules and boundaries to address conflict when it occurs or change the environment in which the two parties work. In some cases, the only way to eliminate a particular conflict is to physically separate those involved, whether transferring one person to another position or location or allowing someone to leave the company.

Recognizing conflict is valuable, as it can produce innovative solutions when utilizing multiple viewpoints. However, tempers can escalate into something worse when people have shorter than normal tolerance levels. Generally, no one wants a fight, especially not one that could be avoided if people took the time or had the information to see the other person's perspective.

When there has not been an ongoing underlying issue, consider what has made this event different from previous ones. Was it the topic? Was it the situation itself? Or was it a personal circumstance outside of work that affected this event?

There are times when I get frustrated with my son. Yet, if I pause and ask him about the background of his actions, I can better appreciate and recognize why he reacted in a certain way. It may have more to do with other things happening in his world. Committing to understanding my son alters how I react, respond, and think about his behavior going forward.

When mediators are hired to resolve conflict, their first job is to become familiar with the background of all parties involved. They do so by talking with both sides to learn all the known facts and determine what each party needs to fully understand. Therefore, whether you are the one helping to solve a conflict or you are the one in conflict with another, seek to immediately determine what facts are known and unknown by all parties involved. Once this becomes a priority, a resolution may be easier than you initially thought possible.

CHALLENGE

Think back to a prior conflict. Would your reaction have been the same if you had all the facts before responding?

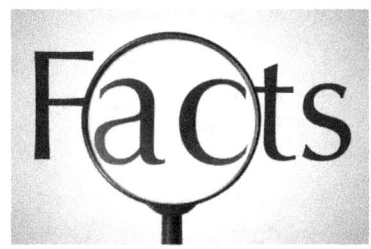

26

Don't Do What Everybody Shouldn't Do

Is this behavior OK for just you?

Your small decisions impact other people.

There are behaviors that you do with little thought which you should stop doing. To find out what they are, test your actions against the question: "What if everybody did this?" If you would not want others adopting the behavior, then you should not either.

For example, a person who uses his phone during a meeting might still be able to listen to the speaker simultaneously. But imagine if everyone in attendance acted this way. How do you think the speaker would feel? Would it negatively impact the energy level in the meeting?

When my kids were in elementary school, they were part of talent shows and musicals. It was tempting for parents to come only for their child's performance and then leave. But if you apply the question: "What if everybody did this?" there would be sparsely attended talent shows with parents coming and going based on whether their child was performing at that moment. This would be disruptive and disrespectful to the other kids, but I have seen it happen. The respectful thing to do is to support all the performers and their families, not only as an audience member but as a fellow parent.

Think about when a timeout is called in sports. Some players listen only passively to their coach's advice during timeouts in the first half of the game. But when a timeout is called in the fourth quarter, it is a different story. They are off the bench and wholly engaged with their coach's advice. They know their focused attention is required if they want to benefit from these strategic insights. Still, they tend to save it for what they view as a more crucial time, such as the final moments of a game. Their lack of attention early in the game hurts everyone on the team.

Chapter 28, entitled "You Can Multitask," may sound like it contradicts this concept. While you can multitask, it does not always mean you should. Multitasking does not grant you the right to be disrespectful. You should not multitask if it is not appropriate for everyone around you to multitask.

People who drive and throw trash out their car windows probably do not ask themselves if it is a good behavior. In the grand scheme of things, what is one piece of trash on the roadside? It may not be a huge disturbance. But what if we all threw our trash onto the side of the road? Could you imagine the eyesore, as well as the negative environmental impact it would have?

Speaking of roads, we could tie this concept into speed limits, too. Speed limits might feel restrictive and illogical because you know how fast you can safely drive. But what would happen if everyone could drive at their desired speed, eliminating speed limits altogether? Getting to work and school every day would become chaotic. Some would go fast while others travel slowly on the same road. Because everyone interprets safe driving speeds differently, accidents would increase... along with fatalities. Hence, while it may not be disrespectful to anyone to drive at a speed you are comfortable with, it would not be logical or safe. So do not do what you do not want everyone else to do.

This principle does not mean you should not ever do something unique. Instead, it suggests you should examine how your small decisions impact others. The frequency of disrespectful behaviors has increased with the adoption of mobile phones. The cell phone offers an instant, real-time source of information and entertainment. This has led to people paying more attention to their phones even when the distraction is inappropriate or unsafe. Once at a church service, the person in front of me spent the entire service on his phone. He believed it was acceptable because he could still listen to the message. But it changed the experience for everyone who noticed his behavior. What if everybody in the church service spent that time glued to their phones? The congregation would be a lifeless, unenergetic crowd, without appreciation or reverence for the sacred aspects of the service, or value of being part of its community.

The cell phone has infiltrated every moment of our lives, tempting us to give it more attention than what is happening around us, even at home. Taking the smallest glance at your phone while at the dinner table can easily become an acceptable behavior and a table-wide issue. What message does this send to your kids? Are there times when they merit your full attention instead? As you use your cell phone, think about what would happen if everybody copied this behavior.

There are several areas in the workplace that would benefit from this principle. You may believe your actions do not harm anyone or anything now. Still those small, seemingly unimportant choices affect so much more than you initially think. For example, what is the harm of taking a few office supplies home for personal use? But what if every employee did this? If you can do it, others will too, which will impact the social standards of the places we work.

Whether it is your behavior in meetings or what you have made a part of your routine at your desk, think about the impact of the hundreds of decisions you make every day. Challenge yourself to positively influence the people around you and commit to consciously not doing what everyone should not do and lead by example.

CHALLENGE

Determine if you have a behavior that everyone should not do.

27

GOLDEN RULE?
OR PLATINUM?

What is the difference between the
Golden Rule and the Platinum Rule?

What are the benefits of the Platinum Rule?

The Golden Rule, "Treat others as you want to be treated," is a universal principle generally respected and followed. However, there may be times when how you want to be treated does not match what others prefer for themselves. Some people reference the Platinum Rule, which is "Treat others as they want to be treated." This forces you to put yourself in other people's shoes and respect their desires. Your consideration for how differently others may express and receive behaviors will benefit both your career and relationships.

With diverse personalities, desires, and values, we all have different ways we want to be treated. Gary Chapman's popular book, *The Five Love Languages*, provides a helpful illustration. It emphasizes how some people feel loved through the use of words of affirmation while others do so when they receive acts of service. Some enjoy accepting gifts, while others want to spend quality time. Suppose my love language is physical touch and I use that when interacting with others whose love language does not match my own. In that case, I will not be able to connect well with them. My actions may even be perceived as disrespectful. But suppose I communicate with someone else through their love language by first learning what that is. In that case, I will be better respected and appreciated.

Adopting others' perspectives is hard when our natural instinct is to react based on our own. You must intentionally learn about other people so as not to apply the same criteria to everyone in your life. You must truly get to know them. It causes you to become disciplined in discovering communication styles that work best for others. Even though the effort is tremendous, the reward is much more significant. Being aware of how others think versus how you process things may require a mental shift and reconstruction of your habits. I discuss a systematic method for changing habits in Chapter 24, "Four Steps to Change a Habit."

Think about what happens when leaders only respond to their teams in their own preferred style. It is only a matter of time before team members begin to disconnect. The team's communication styles have not been used or respected.

When COVID hit our world, employees experienced this when they were forced to work from home, even if it was not their most productive environment. Many companies even initially announced that employees would work remotely permanently. Over time, they adapted their structure and offered hybrid models, as they found only some desire to always work from home.

Fathers and mothers quickly learn they cannot parent every child the same. It is easy to fall into the parenting trap and assume one style fits all. But life is vastly different today compared to when you were a child. How you were once parented or would have wanted to be parented, may not be the best fit for today's child. Parents must consider their children's personalities and needs to communicate well with them, so they each feel understood and respected.

Anyone who has taken personality tests such as the Myers-Briggs or DISC profile can acknowledge this is true for kids and people of all ages. Individuals presented with the same situation will react in different ways. Hence, at our company, we require all interviewees to take the Myers-Briggs and compare their results against current employees. We compare to see not only how they will fit with the team but also to recognize what they can add to it with their unique personalities.

In a me-first society, considering our preferences before others can be all too common. Whether it is toward a spouse, family, or co-workers, it has become second nature to react in ways we prefer for ourselves because that is the cultural norm. Can you imagine what the world would be like if everybody took the time to appreciate how others want to be treated?

Make an effort to appreciate others' perspectives first. Like most things in life, it will not happen overnight, as I discuss in Chapter 33, "Change the World." But the impact it will have on your relationships and you as a person will be profound.

CHALLENGE

Consider a relationship between a co-worker, family member, friend, or neighbor. Do you consider their preferences during interactions? Are you doing what is best for yourself or them? Do you need more "Platinum" in your life?

28

You Can Multitask

There are times when you should and should not multitask.

Realize what tasks complement each other.

The notion that people cannot multitask has become increasingly popular. Studies have emerged over the last few years claiming it is mentally impossible to multitask, and that we can focus only on one thing at a time. This is not true, especially since we multitask all the time. But first, we must define what it means to multitask.

If you believe the theory that says we cannot multitask, how can we walk and talk simultaneously? This is an example of multitasking, especially if you are getting exercise by walking while conversing with a friend.

Some behaviors and actions do not require a singular focus. While the theory against all types of multitasking is readily disproven, a more valuable lesson is learning when it is beneficial to multitask and when it is not.

Some tasks are best accomplished by having a singular focus to increase productivity. They may require the absence of distraction to allow for creativity. These are tasks for which you need to choose not to multitask. However, some tasks do not require a singular focus and can effectively be done in tandem with another activity. The challenge is to make a conscious decision about when it is more efficient to maintain a narrow focus versus multitasking.

If you need to write, this is not a task that allows multitasking. You need to be able to focus. It may require that you turn off your phone so you do not get distracted by texts, calls, and social media. Isolating yourself from other distractions may be critical at times.

However, at other times you can intentionally plan to multitask. You can pair activities that can be done simultaneously. For example, listen to a podcast that utilizes the mind while walking on the treadmill, a relatively mindless activity. I have installed a standing desk above a treadmill at work, so I can walk while completing certain tasks. Throughout the day, I move emails into a "reading" folder that require a long time to read, then I read at night on my home treadmill. While getting my exercise done while working, I end up with more free time because of multitasking.

To take multitasking to another level, consider which of the five senses an activity requires and simultaneously do activities that pair different senses. Could you eat lunch (taste) while enjoying the aroma of your food (smell), while lifting a weight with one hand (touch), while listening to relaxing music (hearing), and while reading an article (sight)? That would be powerful multitasking that could accomplish a lot in an hour at a high rate of efficiency and effectiveness. But that may sound exhausting, so maybe just do two things at once.

When two or more things that need to get done can be strategically combined, you can reclaim time later for doing more of what you love. By making conscious decisions and taking action, you can find ways to multitask effectively while not compromising times when you should not multitask.

Challenge

Determine one way you can do some type of exercise while completing another required task.

29

100% Utilization of Your Mind

**Are you missing opportunities
by underutilizing your mind?**

Small changes can be impactful.

What percentage of beneficial use of your mind do you achieve?

Your definition of beneficial will differ from someone else's and may even be situation dependent. However, challenge yourself to become more aware of how you use your mind. While it is not possible to achieve 100% utilization, you can dramatically improve effectiveness. What could you accomplish in life if you could have 5% more beneficial use of your mind?

Take a look at your current habits and evaluate their influence. Whether it is routinely switching on the TV or checking your phone constantly, habits may be limiting the beneficial use of your mind. Mindless routines create obstacles to achieving better use of our minds.

Driving is one example of a routine activity that normally does not require undivided attention. We can think of other things while paying attention to driving. What percentage of the time while driving do you put your mind to beneficial

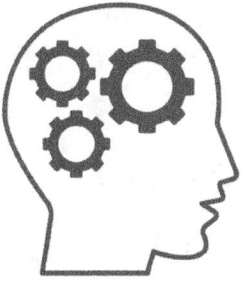

use? Whether you want to contemplate a decision at hand or you want to relax your mind by listening to music, you can make a conscious decision on how to better utilize your drive. Too often we are not intentional and drive mindlessly.

Your mind is powerful. Recognizing you have been using it far too little, will help you use it so much more. Parents will benefit from finding times to increase the effectiveness of their minds, such as thinking through a project versus scrolling on social media while waiting to pick up their child. This better utilization of your mind will free up time later to be present in the moment. Think what might happen if everyone intentionally raised the beneficial use of their minds just a small amount. Collectively, the impact would be extraordinary. See Chapter 28, "You Can Multitask," for specific ideas and recommendations.

Recognize, however, that with increased brain power, there can be an associated level of exhaustion. Not every activity deserves full utilization of the mind, nor should we be occupied with trying to achieve unrealistic expectations.

If you desire to get more out of your life, begin with this one small change. Intentionally focus your mind for better utilization during certain activities or portions of your day. Limit outside distractions during this time. As this principle becomes a natural part of your daily life, you will be pleasantly surprised by the benefits. You will accomplish more of your goals as you improve the utilization of your mind.

CHALLENGE

Select an activity where you can better utilize your mind.

30

TRUTH 100% OF THE TIME

What is wrong with a small inconsequential untruth?

The truth does not have to be hurtful.

People who choose to lie frequently fascinate me. Do they think about what they are doing, or has this behavior become an ingrained habit? While this behavior amazes me, it is unfortunately no surprise in our society where truth has become less important. This chapter is less about dishonesty and more about those who commit to telling the truth but do not follow through with it 100% of the time.

The telling of the occasional white lie often results from believing it is insignificant, unimportant, and in the grand scheme of things, will have little or no repercussions. A one-time partial truth cannot hurt anyone, right? But is it worth questioning your principles because you made them irrelevant in an isolated moment?

The more you hold on to the belief that white lies are harmless, the less conscious and contemplative you will be when justifying future dishonesty, even if it is just 1% of the time.

The most significant negative of even 1% dishonesty is that you are permitting other people to doubt you. They will always wonder what falls within your 99% and what does not. Yes, it is a small percentage, but it makes a powerful difference. It is easier to hold your principles and tell the truth 100% of the time than it is to do so only 99% of the time.

People who do not believe in telling the truth 100% of the time feel that occasionally it is okay to lie because they do not want to hurt someone else. While the truth can hurt, it is more about how and when a message is conveyed than the actual message itself. You should not have to lie for fear of being hurtful. Constructive ways to communicate still allow you to tell the truth.

For example, a wife might ask her husband, "What do you think of this outfit?" He can tell she is proud of what she is wearing. Because he does not want to hurt her feelings, even though he does not feel the same way, he might be

Truth 100%   **Truth 99%**

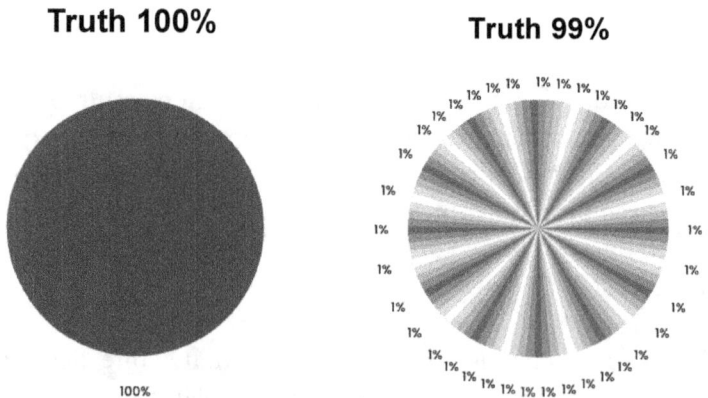

tempted to lie and say, "You look great!" This type of lie will come even easier over time when such a moment presents itself again. As a result, the wife will likely lose trust that he will provide an honest opinion. However, if he were to respond, "You look great in that, but it is not the most flattering outfit that you have," he could have been honest while lovingly sharing his own truth.

When I was growing up, lying was not an option in our house. There were extreme consequences if one of my siblings or I ever got caught lying. It was meant to motivate us to hold the truth in the highest regard. When Julie and I became parents, we adopted a progressive discipline policy for our kids. For the first misbehavior, the child received minor discipline. On the second misbehavior, they received a secondary more impacting consequence, and a progressively harsh discipline on the third. However, if a child lied, they received all three disciplines. The point was that truth 100% of the time was the expectation with no exceptions. When my children might be hesitant to tell us the truth for fear of discipline, I am quick to remind them that lying has the potential to incur more significant consequences in the long run, if not from us, then from elsewhere. You can only lie for so long before it becomes harder to maintain than if you had just told the truth upfront.

This principle also applies in the workplace. If you are the kind of person where the 1% of dishonesty is a reality, there is going to come a point where the people around you no longer will trust you 100% of the time. There will always be the possibility that this time is the 1% untruth. However, suppose you have a reputation for telling the truth 100% of the time, especially when it is difficult to do so. In that case, your coworkers will appreciate this straightforward approach, because they do not have to play a guessing game about the truth of your comments.

Cultivating an environment where truth is demanded, and accepted amidst controversy, allows opinions to have a beneficial impact. If not, team members may reserve their true opinions, even if they would be helpful.

It is important to recognize that telling the truth is not synonymous with saying everything you think. In the 1997 movie *Liar Liar*, Jim Carrey falls under a curse that makes him speak the truth about whatever is on his mind. This results in Carrey making hurtful and inappropriate comments because they come into his mind. There are times when the proper thing to do is to withhold your irrelevant or unhelpful thoughts. There is a difference between deciding the appropriate time for truth and telling a lie. One takes intention and discernment, while the other has superficial appeal with consequences to come. Knowing this difference is not only the key to maintaining truth 100% of the time but will also define your character.

By consciously eliminating lying, you will not have to put in extra effort or muscle memory to keep a lie alive. The truth will never need your help. Mark Twain once said, "If you tell the truth, you don't have to remember anything." While it may appear hard to never lie, if you decide to never lie under any circumstance, it becomes easier to follow your decision. The difference of 1% can be life-changing for you and those around you.

CHALLENGE

Focus on your conversations for one day. Are you 100% truthful?

31

Purpose in Life Changes

What affects purpose?

Do your priorities and actions support your purpose?

What is the purpose of your life? It is a timeless question. The subject has been explored in books and presented in seminars. It has occupied people's time and energy as they hope to discover the answer for themselves. What is so fascinating about the answer is how it changes throughout one's life. There is never only one correct answer to this question. Your purpose at age 20 will not be the same at age 50. As we go through life, our priorities change, we mature, and our evolving perspectives impact how we interpret this important question.

Personal events in life can also influence your purpose. One example is the change in people that experienced a near-death occurrence. These individuals have a much different perspective on life after the event as it causes them to see the fragility of life, and they reset their priorities moving forward. That one instantaneous moment prompted them to change their purpose in life. The change is so dramatic that people who had this type of experience have a much higher divorce rate (65%) [17] because spouses cannot relate to the dramatic change in their partner's approach.

When I was young, I put much thought into determining the purpose of my life. I thought it might be earning money or career achievement, but ultimately I decided it was happiness. As the years went by, my answer changed. I wanted my purpose to be helping others through supporting worthwhile organizations. In essence, my inward-focused perspective shifted to an outward-focused one, changing my definition of success and life's purpose. This dramatically impacted my thoughts, actions, and decisions. When my purpose was about happiness, I made decisions in life that made me happier. When I changed to be about helping others, my happiness became irrelevant, as my choices in life were based on how I could help others. This change may ultimately result in me being happier, but that was not the motivation of my decision. Some people have chosen to die protecting someone else's life. This is an example that their motivation in life was not their own happiness, it was self-sacrifice.

It is crucial to have an open mind when considering your purpose. As you think through your daily actions, how would they change if your goal was to help others rather than to achieve personal success? In our businesses, this mentality dramatically impacts who we hire, how we accomplish our tasks, what the culture is like, and how we work together as a team.

---

17 Sandra Rozan Christian. Doctoral dissertation. Marital Satisfaction and Stability Following a Near-Death Experience of One of the Marital Partners. University of North Texas, 2005.

It even translates into what we do with our profits and, ultimately, what we achieve.

There are so many variables that will impact your definition. It can be dependent upon a particular person, situation, or experience. Because of this, it is a healthy exercise to regularly ask yourself: "What is my purpose?" In Chapter 7, "Focus Days," I talk about having dedicated days to focus on long-term goals. These sessions can be good times to stop and think about your priorities and examine their impact on your life. Start by paying attention to your daily behaviors and evaluate how they are impacted by your decision about what is essential in your life.

CHALLENGE

Determine your purpose at this stage of your life.

empower
service
happiness determination
faith energy family helping balance
share achieve
attitude health teamwork
money community goals
commitment motivation
confidence job discipline

32

LIFE IS ABOUT THE JOURNEY, NOT RESULTS

How should you define success?

How can you enjoy life more?

A person solely focused on achieving results in life misses the joys of the journey. The majority of people define success as achieving predefined goals. I suggest success be rooted in how we run the race rather than what position we finish. This is not to say goals and dreams are not worth striving for because they most certainly are. However, the proper outlook to achieving them needs to be considered more.

I have specific business goals, but because they may change, I do not care if they are met or not. The actions I initiate and the process utilized to reach them matter more to me. I remain focused and work hard to bring my goals to fruition. But I am open to the reality that they could evolve into something else or go unfulfilled for a logical reason. Because of this, I focus on doing what I can now and know that the long-term results may end up meeting my initial goal or, often, something even better.

Focus on the Journey

Not the Destination

I find life more enjoyable when focusing on the journey instead of the results. I can appreciate all the little successes better when I am not so fixated on the larger ones. I also have fluidity in life thanks to this perspective. Each day allows me to set new goals with the freedom to change them without feeling guilty about failure. I recognize that this attitude will not work for particular projects and tasks that must be accomplished. When a goal must be achieved, you do whatever it takes to complete the required tasks since the goal cannot be changed. But keep these types of goals from becoming the dominating activities in your life. If they are, reevaluate and ask yourself: "How am I prioritizing life and organizing my days?"

Consider your business organization and what is believed about the journey beyond achieving results. Our businesses have a Foundation Document about the mission, principles, strategies, and goals. Only one-tenth of it is about goals. The rest prioritizes how we treat people. You can find our Foundation Document at PeakCapitalCompany. com/peak-capital-foundation/. Many businesses' mission statements tend to lean heavily toward achieving specific financial goals. For these companies, the enjoyment of the journey is overlooked at the cost of reaching a financial plan. That is why company culture has become critical for young people to decide where they want to work.

Therefore, set specific goals while maintaining your established principles as you go through life. Always evaluate your actions toward those ambitions, but ensure they are not at the expense of enjoying the journey. Ultimately, personal fulfillment and achievements are about how you run the race, not how you finish.

CHALLENGE

Determine if there are any goals or priorities you need to reassess.

Pick a goal you have set and think about how you can better enjoy the journey toward reaching that goal.

33

CHANGE THE WORLD

What should you do if you do not achieve your goals?

When should you give up?

We all would like to change the world. Individual passions motivate desires in each of us to improve what we see. But our actions to help those causes can quickly result in inward frustration when they do not translate into significant impact. Our efforts can feel like throwing a pebble into the ocean, relatively insignificant, which leads to the temptation of giving up. So why should we even try to change the world? While we typically cannot change the world as a whole, that should not stop us from trying.

Attempting to change the world has a valuable analogy with workplace safety. Large corporations experience several employee injuries every year. But their safety goal for the next year is always zero injuries. While they never achieve their no-injury goal, they keep striving to reach it. Corporations devote significant resources to safety, including equipment, training, and safety leadership positions, despite knowing they will not achieve their yearly goal of zero injuries. Yet, they do not give up. They keep trying.

Trying to change the world is similar. While we rarely achieve our ultimate goal, we should continue to try. In that trying, small positive differences are accomplished.

Like safety, these modest accomplishments have a positive impact, even if they prevent just one injury. It is worth the effort if we can make one small difference in the world. Can you imagine a corporation saying because they will not achieve zero injuries, they will stop trying? It would not make sense. It would also sound illogical to set a yearly goal of only 10 injuries, even if there were 20 the prior year. This would not be an acceptable goal in business and should also not be tolerated in your life. It does not hurt to set a significant goal and go for it. The only negative is if you let shortfalls negatively impact your motivation and you stop trying.

If everybody committed to try to make a positive difference, the world would continually improve. But we know not everyone will work to change the world positively. So rather than get discouraged with what others choose to do, take action in whatever ways you can, and be satisfied with your part.

Some business books falsely imply that if you set big goals, you can achieve them. This may be true for some people, but not all. I suggest you aim for big goals but do not stress over whether they are actually accomplished. Focus instead on your behaviors more than the size of the impact. In the end, you will change the world for the better and often in ways you never imagined.

CHALLENGE

Reflect on a goal you did not ultimately achieve. Reconsider what was accomplished during the process.

Closing

Reading these chapters was easy. Now is the hard part: self-reflection and activation. How have you changed since you first opened this book? What actions have you implemented? Are you taking different approaches to situations? Which chapters do you need to re-read? Have you shared the book with someone who could benefit from it? If you have read this far, you have a passion for self-development and are willing to put in the time to improve. So challenge yourself to think about how you will put the concepts in this book into action.

Download the checklist at:
PeakCapitalCompany.com/33WaysBook

Take time to complete the checklist and set a reminder to review it again in six months. Pick out chapters that will have the most impact in your life and focus on those.

Even after 20 years of developing content for this book, I still challenge myself daily on some of these concepts because I know they will improve my life and the lives of those around me. Whether you are a leader, parent, spouse, co-worker, or work independently, we can all relate to the ideas in this book and can apply them to situations in our own lives.

I would love to hear how the book has helped you.

To send comments, visit:
PeakCapitalCompany.com/33WaysBook

ACKNOWLEDGMENTS

I could not have completed this book without a team helping me. I spent 20 years collecting ideas, but was able to write and publish the book within a year. My son, Chad Myer, did an initial clean-up of the copy. Julia Selwyn then put my words into a better written form. After another round of edits, Wendi Peachey provided a review and edits before it was sent to Demi Stevens for final review. Heather Hayward designed the cover and creative layout.

Only as a team were we able to complete the book. Also, my wife, Julie Myer, was supportive of my book idea and allowed me to take the time to complete the book. Thanks for everyone's help.

ABOUT THE AUTHOR

RONALD MYER is President of Peak Capital. Mr. Myer oversees the operations of each of the Peak Capital portfolio companies and sets a strategy that has provided significant growth in sales and profitability. He leads investment decisions on adding companies to Peak Capital's portfolio. He participated in obtaining an industry-changing patent, negotiating a government multiple award contract (GSA), and obtaining a Qualified Solutions Provider status. Prior to Peak Capital, Mr. Myer was Chief Information Officer for US Plastics Lumber, where he managed 18 people in eight states. He also worked 10 years at Armstrong World Industries, receiving seven promotions within the financial department. He helped grow a division from $34 million to $105 million and was a plant liaison for their SAP implementation and ISO 9000 certification.

Mr. Myer has demonstrated his analytical abilities in helping businesses identify key drivers which lead to increased profitability. His business experience is well-diversified with start-ups, small businesses, and multinational corporations. With over 20 years of investment banking experience, he has facilitated numerous mergers and acquisitions. Mr. Myer is known as a leading change agent with significant involvement in designing and implementing successful corporate restructurings.

Mr. Myer graduated first in class from Auburn University's executive MBA program. He received a B.A. in Management and a B.S. in Computer Information Systems from the University of Scranton and a certificate from Kellogg's Business School on Corporate Strategies for Creating Shareholder Value. Mr. Myer sits on various Boards of Directors.

www.ingramcontent.com/pod-product-compliance
Lightning Source LLC
Chambersburg PA
CBHW060518130626
46553CB00002B/550

* 9 7 9 8 9 8 7 4 0 6 0 0 7 *